# THE WORLD'S MOST SHOCKING SECRETS AND MYSTERIES

KAT HARRISON AND ALLAN HALL

MAKING HEADLINES

Enslow Publishing
101 W. 23rd Street
Suite 240
New York, NY 10011
USA
enslow.com

This edition published in 2017 by Enslow Publishing, LLC.
101 W. 23rd Street, Suite 240, New York, NY 10011



**Library of Congress Cataloging-in-Publication Data**

Names: Harrison, Kat.
Title: The world's most shocking secrets and mysteries / Kat Harrison and Allan Hall.
Description: New York : Enslow Publishing, 2017. | Series: Making headlines | Includes bibliographical references and index.
Identifiers: ISBN 9780766083721 (library bound)
Subjects: LCSH: Curiosities and wonders—Juvenile literature.
Classification: LCC AG243.H25 2017 | DDC 031.02—dc23

Printed in the United States of America



**Photo Credits:** Cover, pp. 1 Pool/AFP/Getty Images; p. 4 Carlos Caetano/Shutterstock.com; p. 7 Carl de Souza/AFP/Getty Images; p. 14 Getty Images; pp. 22, 44, 56 Bettmann/Getty Images; p. 25 Spencer Platt/Getty Images; p. 34 ullstein bild/Getty Images; p. 41 Heritage Images/Hulton Archive/Getty Images; p. 65 Popperfoto/Getty Images; p. 68 Cecil Stoughton/The LIFE Images Collection/Getty Images; p. 76 Laura Pedrick/Getty Images; pp. 79, 90 (inset) © AP Images; p. 84 Ed Jones/AFP/Getty Images; p. 95 Universal History Archive/Universal Images Group/Getty Images; p. 99 US Army via Hiroshima Peace Memorial Museum/AP Images; p. 105 Silver Screen Collection/Moviepix/Getty Images; p. 113 Frank Micelotta Archive/Hulton Archive/Getty Images; p. 122 Jeffrey Mayer/WireImage/Getty Images; p. 128 Vince Bucci/AFP/Getty Images; p. 136 Nova Scotia Archives; p. 142 Imagno/Hulton Archive/Getty Images; p. 147 Nathan Benn/Corbis Historical/Getty Images; p. 155 Imagno/Hulton Fine Art Collection/Getty Images; cover (inset), pp. 6, 30, 61, 81, 104, 133, 157, 158, 159 © iStockphoto.com/Maxiphoto; pp. 11, 12, 46, 73, 74, 89, 90, 91, 124 (map) twobee/Shutterstock.com

# CONTENTS

# INTRODUCTION

Mysteries, scandals, and secrets. They cover the tabloids, newspapers, news shows, and the internet. They spark media frenzies and have been known to ruin lives. And it seems as though no one is immune: musicians, actors, politicians, and even royalty have found themselves part of a mystery or scandal. From crimes of passion, to murders most foul, these scandals and military secrets have rocked the world and changed the world's perception of the people involved.

Here is a collection of the world's unsolved crimes, state secrets that shocked the world, and scandalous affairs that ruined careers. The story of Marilyn Monroe's relationship with President John F. Kennedy. The story of the Watergate scandal that drove Richard Nixon out of the White House in shame, and the secrets held tightly by the North Korean government. The story of disgraced American hero OJ Simpson, and the curse of twenty-seven.

All of these secrets and mysteries caused media stirs and kept the world enthralled as the stories unfolded.

# CHAPTER ONE: CRIME SECRETS

## JACK THE RIPPER

In 1888 the sun never set on the British Empire, with colonies in almost every continent on the planet. But in London, the center of this huge domain, there was a place where the sun never shone. The East End was a disgrace to the empire and to civilized values. People lived in squalor, poverty, and filth. Child deaths were double the national average and prostitution, drunkenness, sexual abuse of minors, and murders were everyday occurrences. It was the sordid environment of a killer whose notoriety lives on unabated to this day. Jack the Ripper made the mean streets of the East End his killing ground. Even now, with the crumbling slums gone, the taverns of those days replaced with offices, cafes, and boutiques, and the gas lamps replaced with electric ones, the East End has become a lurid shrine for Ripper enthusiasts, fascinated by the macabre killer's violent deeds. But the question remains: just who was Jack the Ripper? It is this question of his identity, with all the suspicions that Jack the Ripper may have been someone highly placed in British society, that has made the "Monster of the East End" a creature of intrigue and has ensured his dastardly deeds are never far from the public's mind.

Jack the Ripper may have gone down as history's most famous murderer, but his reign of terror was a short one. He first struck on August 31, 1888. Mary Ann Nichols, a prostitute who served the Whitechapel area of the East End, was found butchered in one of the area's many dark alleyways. "Pretty Polly," as the forty-two-year-old was known, was a chronic drunkard and well-known inhabitant of the taverns in the area.

Police think Mary Ann approached a stranger looking to sell her wares. He lured her into a dark ally, wrapped his hands around her throat, and then cut her from ear to ear. "Only a madman could have done this," said a police surgeon who examined the body later. "I have never seen so horrible a case. She was ripped about in a manner that only a person skilled in the use of a knife could have achieved."

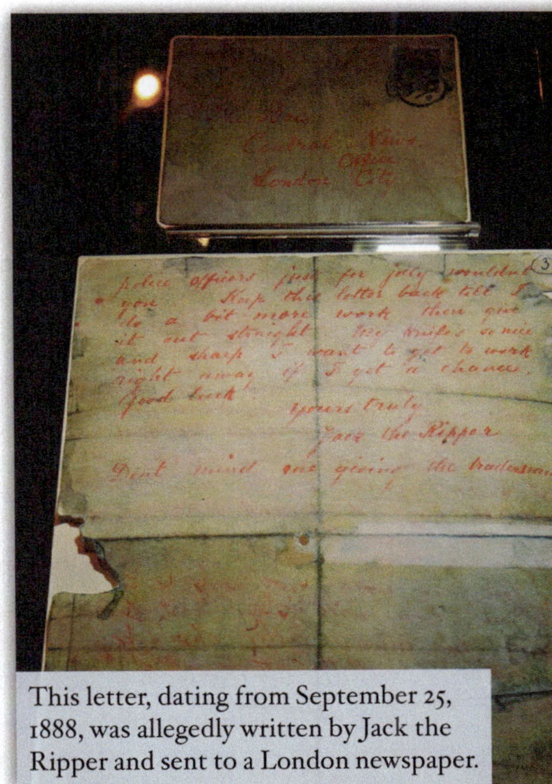

This letter, dating from September 25, 1888, was allegedly written by Jack the Ripper and sent to a London newspaper.

Murders in that area were not uncommon. Police were happy to put the murder down to a single frenzied attack, until just one week later, on September 8, "Dark Annie" Chapman, also a prostitute, was found on Hanbury Street near Spitalfields Market with her few possessions neatly laid out alongside her disemboweled corpse. As with the first murder, there was no obvious sign of rape, but there was every indication that the killer was motivated by some terrible sexual rage as he cut and slashed at the body with grotesque abandon. The dissection of "Dark Annie," her entrails laid out next to her corpse, indicated a knowledge of anatomy or surgery not found in the everyday killer.

On September 25, a mocking letter was sent to a Fleet Street news agency. It read:

*Dear Boss, I keep on hearing that the police have caught me. But they won't fix me yet. I am down on certain types of women and I won't stop ripping them until I do get buckled. Grand job, that last job was, I gave the lady no time to squeal. I love my work and want to start again. You will soon hear from me with my funny little game. I saved some of the proper stuff in a little ginger beer bottle after my last job to write with, but it went thick like glue and I can't use it. Red ink is fit enough I hope. Ha! Ha! Next time I shall clip the ears off and send them to the police, just for jolly.*

The sick message was signed "Jack the Ripper."

Victim number three was Elizabeth Stride, nicknamed "Long Liz" because of her height. A policeman found the body of forty-four-year-old Liz on Berner's Street, Whitechapel, on September 30, near some factory gates. Like the others her throat had been cut from behind, but she did not suffer mutilation or sexual savagery. This led police to think that the murderer had been disturbed in his gruesome work. On the same day they discovered victim number four a few streets away in Mitre Square. Catherine Eddowes, forty-three, was disemboweled and her face practically hacked off.

By the time of this fourth murder, Ripper hysteria had gripped London and was raging faster than the plague in the dark, damp passageways of the East End. Women began arming themselves with knives and whistles to attract the police; the *Illustrated Police News* speculated that upper-class ladies were arming themselves with pearl-handled pistols in case the Ripper was tempted to move up the social ladder in his search for bloody satisfaction.

The Eddowes murder disturbed the police greatly. Her body was by far the most mutilated of all the victims and there was a trail of blood leading to a wall where, scrawled in chalk, was the message: "The Jewes are not men to be blamed for nothing." Sir Charles Warren, the head of the Metropolitan Police Force personally removed the notice and may have destroyed some vital evidence in the process. He was concerned that with the influx of Jews from Eastern Europe into the area this note could have led to savage attacks caused by high racial tension.

The rumors about who the murderer was circulated like wildfire. Some who lived in the East End said it was a policeman on his nightly rounds, his job giving him the perfect alibi to be out at night on those cold, dark streets. One suspect was a Russian-born doctor called Michael Ostrog; it was rumored that he was sent by the Tsarist secret police to stir up hatred against the expatriate Jews who fled from persecution in Russia. Others suggested it was a mad surgeon. Another theory posited that it was Sir Charles Warren himself, a leading Freemason who removed the notice to protect a Freemason killer.

The fifth and final death came on November 9, when Mary Kelly, a twenty-five-year-old prostitute, was grotesquely mutilated in her squalid rented room. On the morning of November 10, Henry Bowers, her landlord, knocked on her door to collect the rent. The previous evening the attractive blonde woman had been seen approaching strangers asking them for cash. The last one she approached, tall, dark, with a mustache and a top hat, was her killer. Bowers saw the remains of Mary and later told police: "I shall be haunted by this for the rest of my life."

Mary's death was to be the last. Nearly 130 years later, the puzzle of the Ripper's bloody but brief reign has still not been solved. It was with the passage of time that more and more people grew intrigued by the Ripper mystery. One suspect who has continued to cause violent debate was Queen Victoria's grandson Prince Albert Victor, Duke of Clarence. He was said to be mad and incarcerated in a mental institution after he had committed the murders because the scandal would have been too great had it ever been revealed to the world. Another theory suggests the Duke had impregnated a prostitute and used the Ripper persona as a way to hide this. Regardless of the motivation, fans of the Duke of Clarence as the Ripper point out that there were no more killings after he was incarcerated.

However, Inspector Robert Sagar, who played a leading part in the Ripper investigation, said before his death in 1924: "We had good reason to suspect a man who lived in Butcher's Row, Aldgate. We watched him carefully. There was no doubt that this man was insane. After a time his friends thought it advisable to have him removed to a private asylum. After he was removed there were no more Ripper atrocities."

But this answer has never satisfied criminologists. Hundreds of suspects have been put forward over the years. One suspect favored by several authors is Montague John Druitt, whose body was found floating in the Thames a few weeks after the murder of Mary Kelly. Those who favor this theory point out that after the impoverished lawyer committed suicide, there were no more slayings. Druitt's family had a history of mental illness and he had acquired basic medical skills as a young man, which points to the possibility Druitt could have murdered prostitutes in such a gruesome way.

Another suspect in retrospect was American quack doctor Francis Tumbletee, who left London shortly after the murders, and who was rumored to have a collection of female body parts in jars.

Other suspects include serial killer Thomas Neill Cream. Although Cream's weapon of choice was poison, upon his hanging at Newgate Prison, his last words allegedly were "I am Jack the..." before his neck snapped and he died. Another suspect is English-born Australian murderer Frederick Deeming, who was in London at the time of the Whitechapel incidents. Some modern criminologists posit that Jack the Ripper was a true nobody, someone that didn't stand out in the crowd, perhaps a butcher who resided in the East End.

## Lizzie Borden

*"Lizzie Borden took an axe. And gave her mother forty whacks. When she saw what she had done, she gave her father forty-one!"*

We have all heard the rhyme on the playground as children. But who was Lizzie Borden? And did she really kill her parents?

That is a secret to which we still don't have an answer, over a century later.

Legend states that the Borden household, at 92 Second Street in Fall River, Massachusetts, was a tense one. Andrew Borden lived there with his second wife, Abigail, and Andrew's two daughters, Emma and Elizabeth (Lizzie). Andrew Borden was known for being rather cheap, refusing to give the house indoor plumbing, and refusing to live in a more affluent area they could easily afford. But he gave gifts to his new wife's family, much to his daughters' chagrin.

On the morning of Thursday, August 4, 1892, both Andrew and Abby Borden were found dead by daughter Lizzie. Abby had been in her upstairs bedroom when she was struck with an axe eighteen or nineteen times. Andrew Borden had been downstairs in the sitting room when he was attacked eleven times with the same weapon.

A maid claims that she saw Lizzie around the house that morning, even heard her giggling once, before discovering the bodies. Had Lizzie Borden, an educated well-to-do young woman, actually killed her parents?

In the basement, police discovered two axes—one with a freshly broken-off handle. Investigators took Lizzie in for questioning. Her story often seemed contradictory, her behavior erratic. At one point she said she was out in the barn looking for a tool. At first she said she'd heard a groan and a loud thud. Then, she said she'd re-entered the house because she didn't think anything was amiss. Certain questions she refused to answer all together. It was noted that a doctor had given her a dose of morphine to calm her nerves, which most likely affected her ability to answer said questions.

A grand jury trial began on November 7, 1892. A few weeks later, Lizzie was indicted, or charged, with her parents' murder. Her trial began on June 5, 1989. Fifteen days later, after an hour and a half of deliberation, the jury acquitted, or cleared, Lizzie.

But did Lizzie get away with murder? No one was ever charged with the murders, and even though she looked rather guilty, other theories were posited by investigators. One suggested Lizzie committed the murders while in a fugue state and was therefore not really responsible. Another theory suggests that Andrew's illegitimate son committed the crimes.

Lizzie and her sister, Emma, moved into a large, luxurious house after the trial, having inherited their father's money. Lizzie became somewhat of a celebrity and enjoyed throwing lavish parties and rubbing elbows with the rich and famous. Her sister preferred a quieter life, and the two moved apart in 1905. Lizzie died of pneumonia on June 1, 1927, leaving all her money to the Fall River Animal Rescue League, taking her secret to the grave with her.

To this day, Jack the Ripper continues to be a point of fascination for the public, inspiring tours in Whitechapel, countless films, documentaries, books, and his own fan club of sorts, called Ripperologists. It is, no doubt, the mystery of his identity that has maintained his rank as one of the most famous serial killers of all time. We may never know the true identity of Jack the Ripper, or what caused him to commit such heinous crimes, and therein lies the fascination with his crimes.

## The Green River Killer

Police said he could be anyone. He could have been a doctor, a lawyer, a mechanic, a shoe repairman. But his secret was one of the darkest in American criminal history: the Green River killer, a demonic monster who killed at least forty-eight women in the 1980s and 1990s. The secret of his success, say detectives, was that he was so unremarkable.

In July 1982 two little boys were out on a fishing trip along the Green River near Seattle-Tacoma International Airport in Washington State. The children were bicycling along with their fishing gear, intent on an afternoon of fun by the river, when one of the boys saw what he thought was a log floating in the shallows, near the iron girders of Peck Bridge. He waded in and rolled it toward himself with his foot before reeling back in horror. He had found the body of sixteen-year-old Wendy Coffield, the first known victim of the Green River killer.

At first, King County police Lieutenant Jackson Beard thought he was dealing with a straightforward murder of passion: a man who had too much to drink picks up a prostitute, becomes violent, kills, and dumps the body.

Wendy Coffield was a prostitute and runaway from a nearby town, who had been missing for three months when she was discovered by the boys fishing on July 15, 1982. Five weeks later a one-time sex crime turned into the beginning of the nightmare.

Gary Leon Ridgway, also known as the Green River killer, plead guilty to the murders of nearly fifty women.

On a single day the bodies of three more young women were found in the river at separate locations, all naked, all strangled, and all showing evidence of having been raped. In these early years of the Green River killings, investigators were able to find fluid samples on three of the bodies. No other physical evidence was ever discovered.

Over the following years the bodies of forty-four more women between the ages of fifteen and thirty-six were found all over King County, in neighboring Northern Pierce County, and in Oregon. Local authorities combined forces with the FBI to create the Green River Task Force in order to apprehend the serial killer. The Green River killer turned lush meadows and lonely woodlands around Seattle into "cluster dumps" for his victims. Bodies were found by mushroom pickers, hunters, joggers, boy scouts, apple pickers, and families camping. In one case an amiable psychic said she was drawn straight to the skeleton of one victim after seeing visions of the dead girl over a seven day period. Investigators felt as though they were weeks, months, if not years behind the killer and began to doubt if they would ever catch up with the most prolific serial killer in American history.

In 1984, investigators got some help from an unlikely source: convicted serial killer Ted Bundy, who was serving his sentence in

Florida. Bundy reached out to police citing that he had particular insight into the Green River killer ("The River Man," as Bundy called him), not because he was a serial killer with a similar victimology, but also because he was from the area where the killer stalked, strangled, and buried his victims. Bundy suggested that the investigators should focus on the dump sites. Bundy said that these places were sacred to the killer, and it was quite evident to him that the killer was revisiting the bodies of his victims. Bundy even went so far as to posit that the River Man was interested in necrophilia. In a stomach-churning turn of events, Ted Bundy would prove right about all of these facts.

But the Green River Task Force didn't just rely on the thoughts of a serial killer. On a few occasions witnesses had glimpsed the victims with strange men shortly before they were discovered dead. From these witnesses, police were able to compile a composite sketch. They also discovered that the killer drove a pickup truck and frequented certain areas of Seattle well known for prostitutes and runaways. Suspects were brought in for questioning. They included cab drivers, truck drivers, gas station attendants, and pimps. But none proved to be the murderous mastermind that investigators were hoping to find.

In 1986, investigators connected these witness statements to a truck painter, Gary Leon Ridgway. One witness identified him in a photo lineup that the police had put together. In 1987, there was enough evidence to get a court order for a search of Ridgway's home and truck and to collect a DNA sample from him. Ridgway, a divorced father of one, seemed so very unobtrusive that investigators doubted the man's guilt in the crimes. He even helped investigators search his home and gave up his DNA willingly, chewing on a piece of gauze. DNA testing and forensic science was a new field and wasn't yet as certain as it is today. Gary Ridgway was set aside as a suspect when his DNA didn't match the degraded samples retrieved from early victims. But police never really let him out of their sight, even though the killings slowed. They monitored his credit card records and all of his various pickup trucks, which he changed the paint color of frequently. They even checked in with his neighbors, who all claimed that Gary Ridgway was the most harmless and friendly of neighbors.

But in 2001, science finally caught up with the Green River killer. DNA testing became the standard forensic evidence in courts across the world, and there were just a few small samples left from the Green River cold case. But when it was tested, there was no doubt: the Green River killer, responsible for the deaths of over forty-eight women, was Gary Leon Ridgway. But who was this man who was capable of killing so many women in such an intimate way without being caught for so many years?

Gary Ridgway was born in 1949 in Salt Lake City, Utah. He had a very average childhood—except for the fact that Gary's mind just wasn't quite right. He showed all the markers of an up-and-coming serial killer. He wet the bed well into his teen years, dabbled in arson, and enjoyed killing animals. He even admitted that at sixteen he'd stabbed a six-year-old neighbor just to "know what it feels like to kill someone." He was sexually aroused by his mother, while also desiring to kill her. He had a low IQ; it took him six years to graduate high school. He married his sweetheart Claudia Craig in 1970 and joined the navy. This time stationed overseas proved to be extremely influential for Ridgway. He frequented prostitutes in the Philippines, where he also was diagnosed with gonorrhea. Upon returning home, he discovered that his wife had been carrying on an illicit affair. These two events brought to light Ridgway's hatred for prostitutes, but it did not make him a killer.

Ridgway remarried in 1972, to Marsha Winslow. At first the marriage seemed perfect for Ridgway. Marsha was doting and was willing to do anything to make her husband happy, including having sex in outdoor locations. They would playfully engage in intercourse along the side of roads, on beaches, and in the forests that would one day become Ridgway's burial grounds. But in 1975, Marsha gave birth to a son, Matthew, and the relationship between the couple changed. Once a loving husband, now Ridgway's affections had taken a creepy turn, including choking and scaring Marsha from behind. They divorced in 1982. He would later tell psychologists that his divorce from Marsha was the "point of no return." Just a few months later, the body of Ridgway's first victim, Wendy Coffield, was discovered.

On November 1, 2002, Gary Ridgway was arrested at the Kenmore Paint facility in Seattle where he worked. At first, Ridgway seemed as compliant as he had with police before. But soon, he realized he wasn't going to get off this time. On November 5, 2003, he pled guilty to forty-eight counts of murder and had to face his victim's families for the first time. He was sentenced to forty-eight consecutive life terms. He was spared the death penalty by agreeing to work with police to locate the bodies of other victims. He has confessed to seventy-one murders, but experts agree it could be as many as ninety or more. He is currently serving out his sentence at Washington State Penitentiary.

Just how many lives did Gary Leon Ridgway, better known as the Green River killer, take? He has admitted he doesn't remember their names or faces, just the places where he buried them. And now he claims his memory has faded. Is he playing a game with authorities? He has little to live for. His third wife divorced him while he was in prison. His son and brothers have all but abandoned him. Perhaps he is toying with police as so many psychopaths do. Perhaps we will never know just how prolific this serial killer truly was.

## The Zodiac Killer

In Vallejo, California, on December 20, 1968, the bodies of a couple were discovered stabbed in their car. Sixteen-year-old

Betty Lou Jenson and seventeen-year-old David Faraday were gunned down on their first date. On July 4, 1969, another couple was gunned down in their car. Twenty-two-year-old Darlene Ferrin was shot five times, while her friend, nineteen-year-old Michael Mageau, survived, despite having been shot several times himself. But what links this crime to the earlier is that the killer actually called the police. The killer reported a "double murder," and then, almost as an afterthought, also admitted "and I killed that other couple." Police traced the call to a phone booth at a nearby gas station, but found the phone off the hook and no fingerprints or other evidence of a murderer having been there. Mageau described the killer as a white man, tall, stocky, with brown curly hair.

On August 1, 1969, the *San Francisco Chronicle,* the *Vallejo Times Herald,* and the *San Francisco Examiner* received mysterious letters that said, "Rush to Editor." The nearly identical letters, claiming to be from the killer, contained a code: eight lines long, each with seventeen symbols. In the letter, he demanded that the letters be printed on the front page of the newspapers the next day or he would drive around killing people, maybe up to a dozen over the weekend. The letter stated that the killer was proud of what he'd done, and that the code, if broken, would reveal who he was.

A week later, another letter arrived at the *San Francisco Examiner.* This one, far more chilling than the first, began with a now famous and haunting line: "Dear Editor. This is the Zodiac speaking." He had given himself a name, and his notoriety grew.

The FBI and many code breakers couldn't seem to break the cryptogram the Zodiac had sent. The code was printed in the newspaper. A high school teacher, Donald Harden, and his wife, Betty, were able to break it. The chilling cipher didn't reveal the identity of the killer. Instead, it revealed his motivation:

I KILLING PEOPLE BECAUSE IT IS SO MUCH FUN
IT IS MORE FUN THAN KILLING WILD GAME
IN THE FORREST BECAUSE MAN IS THE MOST
DANGEROUE ANAMAL OF ALL TO KILL SOME-
THING GIVES ME THE MOST THRILLING EX-
PERENCE IT IS EVEN BETTER THAN GETTING
YOUR ROCKS OFF WITH A GIRL THE BEST PART
OF IT IS THAE WHEN I DIE I WILL BE REBORN
IN PARADICE AND THEI HAVE KILLED WILL
BECOME MY SLAVES I WILL NOT GIVE YOU
MY NAME BECAUSE YOU WILL TRY TO SLOI
DOWN OR ATOP MY COLLECTIOG OF SLAVES
FOR MY AFTERLIFE EBEORIETEMETHHPITI

The last eighteen letters of the code have never been broken. Perhaps they really do reveal the killer's identity. There are several misspellings in the cipher and the letters, and handwriting analysts revealed that the way the killer created his letters, along with his syntax and the many misspellings, pointed to someone with a low level of education.

The cipher also makes reference to "The Most Dangerous Game," a 1924 short story in which a wealthy man hunts humans instead of animals.

On September 27, 1969, Bryan Hartnell and Cecelia Shepard were picnicking on the shore of Lake Berryessa in Napa County, California. Their lovely weekend trip turned into a nightmare when a tall man wearing an executioner's hood and sunglasses pointed a gun at them. He ordered the woman to tie up her boyfriend using the precut lengths of rope he'd brought with him. He then took out a bayonet-type knife and stabbed the couple repeatedly. Then, with a felt-tip pen, similar to the one he used to write the letter, the zodiac scrawled a symbol on Hartnell's car door, along with a message: "Vallejo 12-20-68 7-4-69 Sept 27-69-6:30— by knife."The symbol, known as a zodiac symbol, was a circle with an elongated cross through it.

At 7:40 p.m. the killer called the Napa County Sheriff's office, once again to report his crime.

A local fisherman had heard Shepard's screams and found the couple. Shepard was unconscious and would never regain consciousness. Like in the earlier crime, the male victim, Bryan Hartnell, survived to tell the police about his ordeal.

Shortly before 10:00 p.m. on October 11, 1969, in San Francisco, cab driver Paul Stein picked up a passenger and began driving him to the affluent neighborhood of Presidio Heights. At the corner of Cherry and Washington streets, Paul Stein was shot in the back of the head. Teenagers across the street saw a man get out of the cab and begin to wipe it down. They called the police. A few blocks away a policeman answering the call questioned a white man walking away from the crime scene, but did not detain the stranger. Was this the now-famous Zodiac killer?

Police discovered that part of Paul Stein's shirt had been torn away, and his keys and wallet removed from the scene. The cab was filled with blood, and police discovered a set of fingerprints on the handle of the cab's door. But there was no other physical evidence at the scene. Police weren't even sure this was the work of the serial killer, until three days later, when another letter was sent to the *San Francisco Chronicle.*

"This is the Zodiac speaking," began the letter. The letter went described the killing of Paul Stein and had a piece of the cab driver's bloodstained shirt attached. The killer taunted police and threatened the lives of schoolchildren. It was clear that the killer was enjoying the publicity and notoriety. He enjoyed the fear that he caused to permeate the lives of citizens of Northern California.

A task force was created by the San Francisco, Napa, and Solano County police officers in order to apprehend the murderer. But while taunting letters continued to arrive at local newspapers, the killer didn't take credit for any crimes for several months.

But in March of 1970, a pregnant Kathleen Johns and her ten-month-old daughter were driving to her mother's house in Petaluma, California. A car behind her began flashing its lights and honking. Johns pulled over, and the driver behind her followed suit. The man got out of his car and told Johns one of the wheels of her car was wobbling, and he offered to tighten the lug nuts for her. Thinking the man was a good Samaritan, Johns accepted his help. But as she pulled back onto the highway, her wheel almost immediately fell off. The man offered to drive Johns and her daughter to the nearest service station for help. She and her daughter got into his car. But the driver drove past several service stations and threatened the terrified woman. For ninety minutes, he drove haphazardly along the back roads near Tracy, California. Finally, Johns grabbed her daughter and jumped out of the car and ran into a field, where she hid in the tall grass. The driver attempted to find her, but as traffic intensified, he gave up. Johns hitched a ride from a passing motorist and went to police in Patterson. In the police station, she noticed the composite sketch that had been created using eyewitness recollections. She told the sergeant on duty that the man depicted in the sketch had just kidnapped her and her daughter. This was the last confirmed sighting of the elusive serial killer.

Over the next few years, the Zodiac killer continued to communicate with authorities and journalists. He took credit for many crimes, including the 1966 killing of college student Cheri Jo Bates. Many of his letters kept a sort of score, ending with his symbol and a number of alleged victims. On a letter postmarked January 29, 1974, and sent to the *San Francisco Chronicle*, the Zodiac praised the new film *The Exorcist* as a "great satirical comedy" and included a series of symbols that have yet to be deciphered by the po-

San Francisco police circulated this composite drawing of the Zodiac killer. The serial murderer's identity was never uncovered.

lice. This letter concluded with "Me = 37, SFPD = 0." It was the last letter authorities would receive from the serial killer. If he truly did commit thirty-seven murders, he has only been credited with five murders and two injuries. However, if the Zodiac was telling the truth in his final correspondence, there are an additional twenty eight murders as of yet still unsolved that could be credited to him, which would make the Zodiac the most prolific uncaught serial killer of modern times.

But police must have some idea who he was. They created a task force to find him. So what did their investigation discover? According to handwriting analysts, the Zodiac killer wasn't very well educated. The way he formed his letters, plus his misspellings and phrases, gave him away as someone who likely didn't have more than a middle school education. Although he wrote many things in codes and ciphers, which points to a higher level of intelligence, codes are no good to their readers if they cannot be deciphered.

One suspect that the police questioned time and again was Arthur Leigh Allen. On September 27, 1969, Allen returned to his home in Vallejo covered in blood from a fishing trip on Lake Barryessa. Allen's explanation is that he had run into some friends near the lake and had butchered chickens instead of fishing. A friend of Allen's claimed that Allen referred to himself as the Zodiac. Allen was questioned twice by police. During his first time in police custody, he allegedly volunteered the information that he enjoyed the story "The Most Dangerous Game." He wore a Zodiac brand watch every day, and it was discovered that he loved guns. Allen had subscriptions to several gun magazines, as well as many registered guns in his possession. One of the Zodiac's victims, Michael Mageau, picked Allen out of a photo lineup.

A search of Allen's trailer home in 1972 brought to light other disturbing evidence: a freezer full of dissected animals and several bloody knives. However, Allen's handwriting didn't match that of the Zodiac killer and neither did his fingerprints. His home was searched again and still turned up no evidence related to the murders.

In 1992, Arthur Leigh Allen died of a heart attack. A sample of his brain tissue was saved, in order to be matched against any DNA evidence that might be discovered. In 2000, the Zodiac's letters were examined using new forensic science technology. A partial DNA sequence was discovered on one of the envelopes, and palm prints were discovered on the letters. Neither of these matched Arthur Leigh Allen.

Nearly forty years after his first murder, the Zodiac killer's identity remains a mystery. Some investigators assume he may have gotten himself locked up in prison for unrelated charges, and that's why he hasn't made his presence known since 1970. Others presume the killer is dead. Still others think the killer may be lying in wait for the right moment to reveal himself to the world. Whichever is the case, the Zodiac killer and his murders remain unsolved. And his identity and crimes will go down in history as one of America's great crime mysteries.

## The Long Island Killer (aka the Seaside Killer, aka Gilgo Beach Killer, aka the Craigslist Ripper)

"They're after me. They're going to kill me." Shannon Gilbert's desperate call to 911 in the early morning hours of May 1, 2010, was the last known communication from the twenty-four-year-old escort from New Jersey. She had gone to a gated community in Oak Beach, Long Island, to work for Joseph Brewer, a perpetual bachelor who neighbors say was a known frequenter of prostitutes.

Desperate and terrified, Shannon ran to several houses in the neighborhood, screaming for help and banging on doors. Two neighbors called the police. But by the time police arrived half an hour later, Shannon had disappeared. Investigators at the time assumed she had gotten in the car with her driver, Michael Pak, and gone home. They didn't know how wrong they were.

Shannon's family filed a missing person's report in New Jersey and the search began for the missing girl. Seven months later, as police were searching, a grisly discovery was made: the skeletal remains of a woman wrapped in a burlap sack, barely buried along Ocean Parkway in Long Island. Was this what was left of Shannon?

Investigators and forensic analysis discovered that no, these were not Shannon's remains. Three more bodies, all women wrapped in burlap sacks, were discovered along the same stretch of highway. A few months later, two more bodies were discovered, dismembered and wrapped in burlap. And an even grimmer discovery: pieces of bodies, specifically a female skull and a sack of female bones, brought the body count up to ten. All strangled and mutilated and buried in burlap. But still no sign of Shannon.

The first four victims have been identified. Amber Costello, age twenty-seven, of Babylon, New York, went missing in

September 2010. Maureen Brainard-Barnes went missing in July of 2007. Megan Waterman was reported missing June 6, 2010. And perhaps strangest of all, Melissa Barthelemy, age twenty-four, from New York, went missing in July of 2009. Melissa's teenaged sister, Amanda, received calls from her sister's phone, but instead of a familiar voice, she heard lewd, taunting words from a strange man, telling her exactly what had happened to her sister and what he wanted to do to her.

Investigators determined the second set of bodies discovered was actually older than the first. Of those bodies, only one has been identified. The torso of Jessica Taylor was identified by a tattoo. Her torso had been buried in Manorville, New York. Her head and hands were found later on Gilgo Beach. She had been missing since 2003. The sixth Jane Doe was just a skull, right foot, and hands, also found buried

Investigators comb Long Island beaches after bodies were found nearby in 2011. It is believed that the victims awere killed by the same person.

in Manorville, New York. John Doe, a young Asian man, was discovered on Gilgo Beach dressed in women's clothing. Jane Doe number seven was just a skull and a few teeth. DNA testing determined that her legs had been discovered wrapped in plastic on Fire Island back in 1996. Another Jane Doe, of Latino descent, was discovered not far from the body of a baby girl, who police believe was her daughter. All of the victims appeared to work in the sex trade in New York. And all came to their demise at the hands of one man, investigators say.

Was Shannon Gilbert victim number eleven? What had happened to her that night in May that had terrified her so much that she ran away, desperate and terrified, to awaken neighbors in the sleepy community of Oak Beach? When questioned by police, Joseph Brewer claims he has no idea what "set Shannon off" and that she had simply run out of his house screaming. Michael Pak claims he never touched her and doesn't know what happened to her. But perhaps the strangest part of the girl's disappearance is that her mother also received phone calls. But this time, the man identified himself as Dr. Peter Hackett, a resident of Oak Beach. According to Shannon's mother, Dr. Hackett claimed he ran a halfway house for wayward girls and that Shannon was under his care. When she reported this to the police, Dr. Hackett recanted his story, claiming he never called her. Investigators determined that while Dr. Hackett did indeed call Ms. Gilbert, he was not a suspect in her disappearance, just a wild storyteller who liked to insert himself into investigations.

In December of 2011, police discovered Shannon's jeans, jewelry, and purse in the marsh near Oak Beach. A week later, they discovered the remains of her body face up in the marsh a quarter mile away. Investigators determined that Shannon's cause of death was accidental. In her frenzied and panicked state, she had either drowned or succumbed to the elements. Shannon had been diagnosed as bipolar with a history of depression and violent mood swings. But her family feels that the police are simply not adding up the facts correctly. Many others agree: Shannon Gilbert may very well be the Long Island serial killer's eleventh victim.

The Long Island serial killer, also known as the Craigslist Ripper and the Gilgo Beach killer, solicits his victims online, police say. Many sex workers use Craigslist as a way to generate clients, and it seems that the Long Island serial killer uses this to his advantage. By interviewing family and friends of the known victims, police have determined that the killer lures these desperate women into his clutches with promises of large sums of money, and then he strangles them, dismembers them, and buries them in burlap. No new bodies that have been attributed to the Craigslist killer have been discovered since 2011, but investigators don't think he's stopped. He may have found a new place to bury the bodies. Or he might simply be lying in wait.

There are many other possible victims of the killer. In June of 1997, the torso of an African American woman was found in a green plastic container in Hempstead Lake State Park in New York. The head and limbs were never found, so an identification has never been made, but she has been called "Peaches" by police, because of the tattoo on her breast. On March 3, 2007, a suitcase containing the torso of a Latino or light-skinned African American woman washed up on the beach in Mamaroneck, New York. One of her legs washed up at Cold Spring Harbor in New York a few days later. The day after that, her other leg washed up at Oyster Bay. Both bodies appeared to have been stabbed, which some investigators claim makes neither victim the work of the Long Island serial killer. But other investigators claim that since these bodies were older, this was the early work of the killer, who hadn't yet determined his preferred method of killing.

Another body was discovered by a woman walking her dog in 2013. The remains were intentionally buried and had trauma to the bones. Belonging to an Asian woman in her twenties, investigators believe her body was buried before Hurricane Sandy in 2012.

On June 24, 2013, the remains of Natasha Jugo washed up on Gilgo Beach. She had been missing since March of that year, and her car had been discovered shortly after her disappearance. Although her body was not dismembered, the cause of her death is as of yet undetermined.

Investigators are also revisiting at least two other similar unsolved murders of prostitutes for a possible link to the Gilgo Beach murders.

How is it possible for one man to have killed so many people and gone undetected for so long? The fact is that investigators hadn't been able to link the disappearances of prostitutes together. And in some cases, the missing women weren't flagged as priorities because of their high-risk lifestyles. But now that investigators are on his trail, will they be able to find the killer? Are there more victims out there, waiting to be unearthed or washed up on the shore?

The older bodies discovered were at first linked to another well-known Long Island serial killer, Joel Rifkin. But Rifkin denies having anything to do with the bodies, even though the victimology and manner of death fit Rifkin's modus operandi. But the discovery of more bodies quickly eliminated Rifkin as the perpetrator.

In December of 2015, the FBI joined Suffolk and Nassau County police departments to create a task force dedicated to catching the murderer. They say the killer is most likely a white male in his thirties or forties who is from Long Island and very familiar with the area. He may have ties to law enforcement, which has helped him evade capture. He is most likely an unassuming man. A neighbor. A business owner. A family man. A mechanic, doctor, or lawyer. But one thing is certain: he is out there on Long Island, biding his time until he can kill again.

As for the families of his victims, they finally have some closure. But knowing that their loved ones went from missing to murdered is no solace. And knowing there may be more bodies buried in the Long Island marshes is a terrifying prospect.

For now, the identity of the Long Island serial killer, aka the Craigslist Ripper, aka the Gilgo Beach killer, remains elusive and unknown. No one knows who he is, where he is, or what he's doing. No one knows for sure how many lives he has claimed or how many more victims are out there. But one thing is known for certain: there is a murderer loose on Long Island. And he won't stop until he gets caught.

# CHAPTER TWO: STATE SECRETS

## The Eichmann Affair

After the KGB, the CIA, and MI6, one agency stands out as the most capable, cunning, and ruthless of the smaller intelligence networks in the world. Mossad is an organization dedicated to the preservation of Israel. Its operatives and agents are more than employees—they are disciples of the state of Israel and understand that the maxim of "know thine enemy" applies more rigorously to them than to any superpower. Mossad lives by the creed of a German-born Jewish scientist named Charles Proteus Steinmetz, a pioneering electrical engineer. He once wrote: "There will come an age of small and independent nations whose first line of defense will be knowledge." That has become the motto of the Mossad and indeed it could be said to be the motto of the entire Israeli nation. By staying one step ahead of its enemies, Israel has survived and flourished as the spiritual home for the world's Jewish population.

But it was one spectacular act that earned Mossad the admiration of global spymasters. A top-secret operation concerned not with the security of Israel, but an act of revenge and atonement for the years the Jewish people suffered during the Holocaust. Mossad tracked down and kidnapped one of the most wanted Nazi war criminals.

Mossad was born out of the pre-independence days when Jewish guerrillas fought British colonial rule in Palestine. The Haganah, the underground army formed by the Jewish settlers in Palestine, spawned five intelligence branches during the struggle for independence. One of them was the Mossad—in Hebrew, the Institution for Intelligence and Special Assignments. The primary task of the agency, reformed and restructured after the war of independence by prime minister David Ben-Gurion, was to discreetly complete Israel's dirty and undesirable tasks.

Isser Harel was the first chief of the Mossad. He knew no fear and had no boundaries in his mission to serve the state. More than any other individual he is credited for making Mossad the organization it is today. Harel showed cunning and coolness from the first day he landed in Palestine, smuggling a handgun that he had pledged to put to good use in the fight for a Jewish homeland past the stringent British customs.

After a dedicated war against the British forces, Harel was rewarded with the command of Shin Beth, Israel's second major intelligence service concerned with internal security. Harel put his heart and soul into the Shin Beth and within two years, in 1958, he assumed command of all Israeli intelligence operations.

Isser Harel's obsession with secrecy was something of a joke even within the ranks of the Mossad. A popular gag about him was: "Did you hear about the time Isser jumped into a taxi and the driver asked him where he was going? Isser replied: 'It's a secret.'" But the apparent frivolity masked a devotion to their boss which was second to none. His height of 4 feet 8 inches (142 centimeters) was no drawback; only to the public was he "Isser the Little." To the agents who knew and worked for him he was "Isser the Giant." For a decade he was Israel's chief spymaster, ruling with an autocratic hand. He answered to no one, not even to justify the Mossad budget to Israeli parliament. Such secrecy guaranteed him the intelligence coup of the century and earned him a place in history.

Ricardo Klement was an ordinary man. He went to work at the same time each day, bought his wife flowers on her birthday, and was nice to his children. In Buenos Aires there was nothing to distinguish him from the countless other foreigners who made up the population of this gracious city, often dubbed "The Paris of South America." He was of German extraction, but then so many were; like the British who shopped at Harrod's in the city, they built their own community, embracing the best of the old world and the new. But Ricardo Klement had a secret. In Germany, between 1933 and 1945, he was Adolf Eichmann. And his job had been mass murder.

Eichman had enjoyed the patronage of the highest echelons of the Nazi party. He was a member of the feared SS, rising to the security section of the organization to control the "Final Solution," Hitler's euphemism for the extermination of the Jews. Eichmann was the planner. While the dregs of humanity may have pulled the triggers and herded the unfortunate victims into the chambers, Eichmann was the controller—the man who lent intellectual credibility to the monstrous master plan. Six million people died as a result of his planning, making him the biggest mass murderer in history. And he had escaped justice at the end of World War II.

In 1957, a blind Jew living in a suburb of Buenos Aires heard from his daughter that she was being courted by a man who called himself Nicholas Eichmann. Something triggered itself in the old man's mind; perhaps that this could be the son of the infamous Adolf. He contacted a friend in the German police department who put him in touch with Fritz Bauer, the public prosecutor of the German province of Hesse. It was Bauer who subsequently delivered the news to Isser Harel in Tel Aviv— one of the top ten war criminals still at large might have been found. It led to an extraordinary meeting between Harel and David Ben-Gurion.

"I would like permission to bring Eichmann back to Israel," requested Harel.

"Do it," replied the prime minister.

And with those words, he had sanctioned the boldest intelligence mission in peacetime of the twentieth century.

Not only was the mission unprecedented in its scope, but the implications of its successful (or failed) execution were enormous. Harel was not asking for the extradition of Eichmann, trusting the Argentine government. He had known too long that South America was a common destination for Nazi fugitives fleeing from the ruins of World War II. Harel planned to kidnap Eichmann and bring him to Israel for trial—a mission so secret that one breath of it would have spelled its end and disgraced Israel in the eyes of the world. No matter that they were after a war criminal. Harel knew that the worst crime in diplomatic and political eyes was the one of being caught.

He assembled a hand-picked team of volunteers within the ranks of Mossad, and in early 1958 an agent was sent to Buenos Aires on a reconnaissance mission. He checked out the address that the old Jew had relayed to them, 4621 Chacabuco Street, in Olivos, a Buenos Aires suburb. Nothing. The family of Klement no longer lived there. All the agent managed to gather was that a man whose physical traits resembled those of their quarry used to reside there, but his name was Klement. That meant nothing to Israeli intelligence.

It was not until 1959, after a Mossad agent paid a discreet visit to the elderly Jewish man, Lothar Hermann, that a detailed dossier was built up on the man they thought was Eichmann. Lothar recalled, with a precise attention to detail, the speech patterns and voice of his suspect as well as the physical attributes as they were told to him by his daughter. He also recalled one time when young Nicholas

Nazi leader and SS officer Adolf Eichmann stood trial for crimes against humanity in 1961.

Eichmann had stood in his house and boasted about his father's war service.

A small team of crack Israeli agents, armed with the information supplied by Hermann, stayed on in Buenos Aires. But the budget of Mossad was not then vast enough to expend large amounts of cash without the likelihood of firm results. Harel was on the brink of cancelling the whole operation in December 1959 when an agent picked up a lead. After trailing Nicholas Eichmann from a motorcycle repair shop to a suburb in the San Fernando district of the city, they were sure they had their quarry. But how sure? The Mossad team had the words of a blind lawyer and a seventeen-year-old photo from SS files. They staked out the suspect's house on Garibaldi Street.

The residence was secretly photographed from every angle. More agents were brought in from Israel. The balding and bespectacled man did not know he was the subject of such a manhunt. He didn't know his every action was being monitored by Mossad agents, seeking proof positive that Ricardo Klement was really Adolf Eichmann.

On March 21, 1960, Ricardo Klement got off the bus near his home, clutching a large bouquet of flowers. From the house came the sound of laughter and the beginnings of a party. A woman greeted him warmly at the door. One of the agents watching the shabby house looked in his file and discovered that March 21 was the twenty-fifth wedding anniversary of SS Colonel Herr Adolf Eichmann. They had done it. They had found one of the worst war criminals in history.

After that events moved rapidly. A team of full-time agents was established in Buenos Aires under the on-the-spot command of Isser Harel, who felt he had to take full and personal charge of the operation.

The plan was, in effect, simple. A travel agency was set up in a European city to process the travel documents and permits for the Mossad team to travel to Argentina. The group's overriding concern was not to be publicly seen as violating the sovereignty of a friendly nation. There was no other way, however, than a covert mission. Argentina had long given sanctuary to Nazi war criminals and an official approach, while it might have met with courtesy and public promises of action, would have led to the fugitive escaping even further abroad. Isser Harel would not let that happen.

In Buenos Aires, safe houses were rented all over the city. Agents processed by the travel agency flew in from various European cities. On May 11 it was decided to snatch Adolf Eichmann.

There were tense moments outside the house on Garibaldi Street that night. Failure meant disgrace in the eyes of the world. Every agent positioned in their safe houses and outside the home of Eichmann knew that if the plan went wrong they could count only on their own resources to get clear. The Argentine government had no idea of their plan and would not likely help any Mossad agents out of the country.

In succession, the three buses that Eichmann usually caught coming home pulled up. All the passengers disembarked, and then the buses drove away. But Eichmann was not spotted. On that night the Mossad agents prayed that he had not been tipped off and fled as so many other Nazis had.

At 8 p.m. another bus arrived and Ricardo Klement/Adolf Eichmann stepped off. The secret mission of the decade was on.

Eichmann wandered to the door of his home with the same nonchalance that he usually displayed . He passed a car that appeared to have broken down with two men studying the engine. He did not know that a third man was lying on the floor of the vehicle or that the car parked on the opposite side of the road was positioned to shine its lights directly in front of the parked vehicle. When he got near it he was sandwiched between walls of light that temporarily blinded him. The man on the back seat of the car jumped out and, with the aid of the accomplices studying the engine compartment, bundled Eichmann into the back seat. Holding a pistol to his head, they managed to drive away unnoticed.

An hour later, Eichmann was in one of the safe houses that the agents had rented. Shackled to a bed, "Ricardo Klement" was stripped of the identity that had shielded him from justice for fifteen years. The agents checked under his armpit for his SS number, but found only a scar. But there was no pretense any longer. The bald man who had devised the timetable for the final solution stood in the pajamas that the Mossad had bought for him and said: "Ich bin Adolf Eichmann." *I am Adolf Eichmann.*

After the enormity of their capture hit them, many of the Mossad agents were overcome with emotion. They had all lost loved ones in the Holocaust, which Eichmann had kept running smoothly and on schedule. Many said afterward that they expected a monster, but what they got was a faceless, balding bureaucrat who recited to them in perfect Hebrew the most holy of Jewish prayers.

Eichmann was kept in the safe house for over a week while phase two of the operation was organized— how to get him out of Argentina.

Harel played a hunch during this period. He thought that the family of Eichmann would go through the usual procedures of attempting to find Ricardo Klement: the hospitals, jails, and private clinics. But he suspected they would not contact official channels and raise the alarm for a man who was wanted for some of history's most heinous crimes. And he was right.

Soon, however, the Nazi underground was whispering that something unpleasant must have happened to Comrade Eichmann. That was bad news for Israel. Dr. Josef Mengele, also known as "Dr. Death," who had carried out grotesque and inhumane experiments on inmates at Auschwitz, was able to escape because of those whispers.

But getting Eichmann out of Argentina was the most serious obstacle.

Finally, Isser Harel risked all on a simple ploy. He drugged Eichmann, dressed him and his agents in the uniform of El Al, the official airline of Israel, and arranged for a jet to be at Buenos Aires airport. He explained to the customs officer that his drugged cohort had sampled too much Argentine hospitality the night before, and asked permission to board the aircraft. "He's not flying in that state, is he?" asked a customs officer. "Oh no, we're only the reserve crew," Harel replied. And just like that, they were out of Argentina and on their way to Israel.

Twenty-four hours later in Tel Aviv, "Isser the Little" walked into David Ben-Gurion's office and announced: "I have brought a little present for you."

The following day Ben-Gurion made the most moving speech he has ever made to the Israeli parliament, the Knesset:

> *I have to announce that a short time ago one of the greatest of Nazi criminals was found by the Israeli secret service. Adolf Eichmann, who was responsible, together with the Nazi leaders, for what they called "The Final Solution of the Jewish Problem"—that is the extermination of six mil-*

*lion Jews of Europe. Adolf Eichmann is already under arrest in Israel and he will shortly be brought to trial in Israel.*

The rest is history; Adolf Eichmann, who praised his captors from the dock, was found guilty of war crimes and sentenced to death. He was hanged for his crimes. His one life did not undo the six million lives he took. But it certainly helped Isser Harel feel better.

## The Rosenbergs

The date was June 19, 1953. Old Sparky, the name given to the electric chair in Sing Sing prison, was being tested by Joseph Frankel, who lived near the infamous jail in Cairo, New York. "Electrician Joe," as he was known, was due to collect $300 for his night's work— sending a pale skinny man and his wife to their maker. In his time, Joe had plunged the switch and sent the electricity surging through the bodies of countless Mafia hitmen, rapists, robbers, and murderers. But tonight was different. Tonight Joe was making history as he threw the switch that would send Julius and Ethel Rosenberg into oblivion. They were hated spies who sold out their country to the communists at a time when the Cold War was at its coldest. The only enemy agents ever to be executed in the United States in peacetime.

Shortly before midnight Joe placed the electrodes on Julius Rosenberg's head, strapped the other electrodes to his chest and arms, and placed a leather hood over his face. Two minutes and forty-five seconds later, with smoke still in the air, the traitor was pronounced dead. After a few minutes to clear the air, his wife was brought in and the ghastly scenario was repeated. After four minutes and thirty seconds she too was pronounced dead. The Rosenbergs, two of the Kremlin's most valuable agents, who had buried themselves deeply in ordinary suburban life, paid the ultimate price for their treachery.

The outward appearance of the Rosenbergs was no different from thousands of other US citizens of Russian-Jewish descent. Both were raised in a close-knit community on the Lower East Side in New York City, an ethnic melting pot that encompassed people of practically every race on earth. They were poor but, by all accounts, well loved. Ethel became a clerical worker after graduating from Seward Park High School. The freckle-faced but stern-looking Julius once nurtured a desire to become a Rabbi, but opted instead for an engineering course at the City College of New York in Manhattan.

The couple married in 1939, before the outbreak of World War II, which would see the Germans marching over Europe. In 1945 Julius joined the Army Signals Corps, where he earned $50 a week inspecting electrical equipment. It was an easy job and one that didn't require him to see active service overseas. He lived with his wife in Greenwich Village, and they had two sons, Michael and Robert. Always financially insecure, the Rosenbergs made do like thousands of others and managed to muddle through with the dream that one day things would be better. But they were different from the majority of other Americans. They were communists. They believed whole-heartedly in the international socialist doctrine preached from Moscow. To them it was more than a political movement. It was a religion and a way of life.

Julius had been a communist from his earliest days in college. He was clever enough to keep the fact quiet. The United States had always been the most stridently anticommunist nation in the world. His secret membership in the US Communist Party cost him his job in 1945, when a routine FBI investigation of personnel proved his allegiance to Moscow. With a family to feed, he opened up his own business, Pitt Engine Products, in the same building as a synagogue in downtown

New York City. The venture was plagued by bad cash flow and poor management. But Julius struggled on, and eventually made the fatal mistake of selling state secrets in order to not only aid communism, but also, to aid himself and his family.

Julius Rosenberg, together with his wife and brother-in-law, David Greenglass, sold the United States' most prized secret to the Soviet Union—the formula for the atomic bomb. It was the most heinous of crimes against a state that had assumed the role of free-world protection.

David Greenglass was seized by the FBI on June 15, 1950. He was held and questioned at length. Greenglass worked at the top-secret Los Alamos site in New Mexico during the war years making "lenses"—the detonators for the atomic bomb. Everyone that produced the atom bombs that wiped out Hiroshima and Nagasaki went through a security clearance in case of alien loyalties. Greenglass had somehow slipped through the net.

He stole detailed drawings of the atomic bomb from Los Alamos, along with copious notes of how it worked, how it was assembled, and what was required to make it. His do-it-yourself atom bomb secrets were fed directly through Julius and Ethel to emissaries from the Soviet Union in the United States and back to the Kremlin in Moscow. Greenglass was caught as part of a wide-reaching FBI probe and, in a cowardly attempt to save his own skin, readily implicated his sister and brother-in-law.

It turned out that a rather pathetic Swiss immigrant named Harry Gold, who was the US courier for another major spy, was the go-between for the Rosenbergs and Greenglass. He would meet Greenglass using a code procedure worked out by Rosenberg. At a secret rendezvous point Gold would hand Greenglass the top of a jelly packet with the words "I come from Julius" written on it. This meant that the coast was still clear and that the Rosenbergs required more information to pass on to their Soviet spymasters.

Ethel and Julius Rosenberg were executed for conspiracy to commit espionage. Although doubt surrounded their case for years, it is believed that the couple were indeed rightly convicted.

The United States led the world in nuclear research and had overtaken the Nazis in the race for atomic supremacy. Selling the secrets of their technology was just about the worst crime that they could have committed, especially as it was discovered in the McCarthy era, when witch hunts were conducted to root out everyone and everything deemed to be left-wing and un-American in their actions, deeds, and thoughts.

Gold, who worked as a chemist in Philadelphia before he became embroiled in espionage, was also the courier for top spy Klaus Fuchs. Fuchs was born in Germany and became a communist in his teens. When Hitler came to power he fled to England and became a citizen. He was part of the British mission given top-level clearance to witness research and tests on the bomb. He too used the services of Gold and confessed to spying in 1950, receiving a fourteen-year prison term. To this day it is not known whether he worked independently of the Rosenbergs or with them.

Another person indicted with the Rosenbergs was Morton Sobell, once Julius Rosenberg's classmate at college, who passed on secrets to the couple about the latest radar technology he worked on for the US Navy.

The arrests came in 1950. First Julius in July and his wife twenty-five days later. The FBI file on the Rosenbergs and the others in their spy network comes to some forty thousand pages. It chronicled the information they had channeled to Moscow from 1940 to 1948. At their trial it was claimed that their acts of treason alone had given Russia the atom bomb. Russia exploded their first A-bomb in 1949 when American intelligence had estimated that it should have taken at least fifteen years to catch up in the nuclear race. Thanks to the Rosenbergs' misty-eyed idealism, the Russian bear was armed, ready for the Cold War and the buildup of ballistic missiles.

The fifteen-day trial in 1951 was a sensation that riveted the world. Gold's testimony particularly damned the couple as he told of the secret rendezvous he kept with Greenglass. And Greenglass in turn showed no emotion as he poured out the details of the secrets that would send his own sister and brother-in-law to the electric chair. Although he passed the secrets of the bomb on to Julius, he said his sister was a willing coconspirator who was glad to play her part in ending "world fascism." He said she often stayed up late at night and typed up the careful notes that would be passed on to their Soviet controllers.

Another star witness was Elizabeth Bentley, who testified for the government. A Columbia University graduate, she told how she was lured into the ranks of the communists through several disastrous love affairs with Soviet agents. Though without direct knowledge of the Rosenbergs' activities, she nevertheless played a crucial role for the state in its conspiracy charges against the couple, by testifying that all communists were harmful to the United States because their loyalty lay with Moscow alone.

The jury was convinced and returned with guilty verdicts. In their eyes, the Rosenbergs, who maintained their innocence throughout the trial, conspired to commit espionage against the United States in time of war. They were given the death penalty by Judge Irving Kaufman, who branded them "despicable traitors" and, rightly or wrongly, said their actions had led to the Korean War in which fifty thousand Americans lost their lives. He said Julius had been the "prime mover" of this "diabolical conspiracy" and Ethel was "a fully fledged partner."

Morton Sobell got a thirty-year sentence, of which he served sixteen. David Greenglass, who stole the secrets but did not pass them on to the Soviets directly, was treated remarkably leniently, receiving a fifteen-year sentence, which he served, and then was released. Despite twenty-two appeals and stays of execution, Julius Rosenberg, thirty-five, and Ethel Rosenburg, thirty-seven, died for an administration that demanded blood for the betrayal of its mightiest secrets.

After the switch was thrown that night and the Rosenberg children were adopted by another couple, the doubts and inquests on their guilt or innocence were raised around the world. In Cuba, the Castro regime issued commemorative stamps bearing their portrait and the legend that they were "assassinated" by the United States government. But those close to the case, even a human rights lawyer who detests the death penalty, remain convinced that the quiet couple who beavered away by day in the machine shop were, by night, agents in a far more murky, more lethal world. "It is a ghastly and shameful episode," said top Yale law professor Alexander Bickel, "but I believe they were guilty." Roy Cohn, the prosecutor, said: "I feel the guilt was proven overwhelmingly and has stood the test of time." In 2008, Morton Sobell, who had always maintained his innocence, confessed that he and Julius Rosenberg had indeed been Soviet agents.

Only one man's conscience and heart was not touched by the deaths of the Rosenbergs. For Joe the electrician it was just another job, albeit a celebrated one, among the 137 he carried out before he retired from Sing Sing.

## Mata Hari

Mata Hari was the most famous of all female spies: using beauty, seduction, and sexuality to squeeze secrets from men who might

Mata Hari was an entertainer who used her talents of seduction to spy for the Germans during World War I.

have withstood any torture, save that inflicted by a lovely woman's charms.

Mata Hari was born in the Dutch town of Leeuwarden on August 7, 1876, as Margaretha Geertruida Zelle. She had an ordinary childhood, was an ordinary student, and made the same moans that most teenagers do when they long to do more exciting things. When she was eighteen she moved to a teacher's college near Amsterdam.

But Margaretha quickly tired of studying and, a year later, married an army officer who took her off to Java. It was here that she first heard the native name Mata Hari, meaning "eye of the day," the name under which she would sell military secrets and the name under which she would die.

For the next seven years, Margaretha lived the life of an upper-class colonial woman. But she was acutely aware of her own beauty. She became involved in a few romantic dalliances, which proved to her that her seductive charms could win her anything she wanted. Her husband found out about her affairs, but played the part of a cuckolded husband well. He tolerated Margaretha's infidelity for a number of years before taking her back to Holland, where they separated and later divorced.

Margaretha found herself with little money in 1902. She decided to take up the one thing that had been attractive to her as a teenage girl: dancing. She was a very provocative performer, and the dancing was considered strictly for men. But Paris, rather than Holland, was the place to be in cabaret and theater. So in 1905 she moved to the French capital to continue her dancing—and her love affairs.

In her theatrical life in Paris, she adopted the name Mata Hari. History is blurred on her days in Paris, but it is well known that she had many lovers, most of them military officers. Such dalliances were to damn her when the Great War arrived and the world was divided into armed camps. She stayed in Paris as the Kaiser's forces were locked in stalemate with the allied armies on a broad front stretching from the channel ports to the frontier of Switzerland.

In 1916, Mata Hari moved back to neutral Holland, and it was there that she moved on from dancing to espionage. She fell into the bed of a German diplomat who asked her for details of the French armies in two vital sectors; one was the Somme front where an Anglo-French offensive was expected. The other was at Verdun, which had been heavily fortified and ringed by steel and concrete constructions. The diplomat promised her cash.

The French were later to claim that Mata Hari gleaned the secrets of the French strengths from her lovers in the French Army. She was betrayed to the French authorities in 1917, after she had gone to Paris to pass on some intelligence about French battle plans to a Prussian officer. In a war that was bleeding France, she was tried, sentenced to death, and executed on October 15, 1917, by a firing squad.

What were the secrets that she had passed on? Certainly news of Verdun and the Somme offensive could be deemed to be damaging to the war effort of the Allied nations. But European capitals were full of agents, and the Somme offensive was certainly no secret to the Germans who knew about it months before it began. So who was it who betrayed Mata Hari?

## Wikileaks

In 2006, a group of hackers, led by Australian-born hacker and computer programmer Julian Assange, began to publish news leaks and classified information from anonymous sources. For the next three years, the information was mostly targeted at Europe and Australia. But in 2013 Wikileaks published a series of classified and sensitive military and diplomatic documents about the US government, gained through a former US Army private E-class. These documents included an Iraq War log, as well as files on Guantánamo Bay prison in Cuba. Videos released revealed US attacks on civilians in Iraq.

Soon after, US authorities began investigating Wikileaks and Assange personally. Although the government denies that there is an indictment out for Assange, another leaked document in 2012 reveals that there is (or at least there was at the time). As of 2015, there is an ongoing investigation into Assange and Wikileaks.

As for Assange, he is currently living safely in Ecuador with political asylum, following allegations of a sexual assault in Sweden. Assange vehemently denies such allegations, but he has yet to return to Europe or the United States. It is very likely he will stay as a political refugee for the rest of his life, thanks in part to the many secrets from around the world that he and his organization have revealed.

Assange views this as the price he has to pay for revealing the truth to the citizenry of the world. "If wars can be started by lies, peace can be started by truth."

Since 1917, historians have been puzzled about the whole affair; particularly the French government's refusal to allow public scrutiny of papers about Mata Hari sealed in 1917. But in 1985, a US journalist, Russell Warren Howe, claimed he was shown the secret papers of the spy Mata Hari at the Chateau de Vincennes, the very place where she was executed. He claims that the papers show she was not a German agent, but a freelance "operative" whose sole espionage effort was in Madrid working for the French. Howe says she seduced a German military attaché there and spent three days in bed with him, but the information she got was stale or inaccurate.

Howe claims Hari did accept money from German intelligence, but all she gave them were easily culled newspaper reports and old gossip. But during the Great War, France was rife with anti-foreign sentiment and had suffered appalling losses. Inept generals were to blame, but a scapegoat in the form of a conniving woman with questionable morals seemed a far better bet. At her trial she was charged with peddling secrets which cost the lives of hundreds of thousands of Allied servicemen. And the Germans, who believed that Mata Hari had cheated them as a double agent, sent messages in a code which they knew the French had broken, implicating her in the espionage charges.

Whichever story is true—that she was a German spy, a French spy, or both—Mata Hari broke the ground rules of espionage in that she was indiscreet and naive enough to think that her bed-hopping would not alert informers. Who actually informed on her is, to this day, still a secret.

## Watergate

On June 17, 1972, five men were arrested during a break-in at the Watergate complex in Washington, DC. The Watergate complex housed apartments, offices, and a hotel. The story wasn't big news at first. It was simply seen as a break-in. The men were found with $2,300 in sequential bills, and officers assumed it had something to do with money laundering or counterfeiting. The investigation was turned over to the FBI. Junior staff writers for the *Washington Post,* Bob Woodard and Carl Bernstein, were assigned to write a story about the break-in for the local section of the paper. What the journalists didn't know at the time was that they were about to break the biggest story of political scandal in modern US history.

The five men, Bernard Barker, Virgilio Gonzalez, Eugenio Martínez, James W. McCord Jr., and Frank Sturgis, were all former CIA operatives. While this in itself was curious, their true intentions were not discovered until months later. As the FBI continued to probe into the men and their break-in, it was discovered that the five men had close ties to the White House and its current administration led by Richard M. Nixon.

A year earlier, a devastating blow had been dealt to the government in the form of released political documents, called "The Pentagon Papers." This series of documents, released by Daniel Ellsberg, were a study of government involvement in the conflict in Vietnam. The Vietnam War had devastated the American people. It was the first war shown in full color on television sets in every American home. Many young men were drafted to serve in the conflict and thousands were dying over a conflict that many American people thought was unjust. Many top-ranking officials had told the public that all efforts were being made to minimize the conflict in Asia. What the Pentagon Papers revealed was, in truth, that the US military had secretly enlarged the conflict by bombings in nearby Cambodia and Laos, as well as raids and Marine Corps attacks in North Vietnam, all of which had been kept from the American public, as well as Congress. This revelation turned an already divided American public firmly against their political leaders and the war in Vietnam.

President Nixon, who had inherited the war from former president Lyndon B. Johnson, called the release of these documents "the most massive leak of classified documents in American history." And he wasn't wrong. But his reaction to the release of these papers was. Nixon became paranoid. He hated reporters and the media, considering them enemies. In fact, Nixon considered many people his enemy. From politicians, journalists, writers, and even celebrities who openly opposed him or the Vietnam War, Nixon had a long list of individuals he wanted to keep an eye on. And so he created a secretive group whom he called "the plumbers." The job of these "plumbers"? To stop leaks from the White House to the press. Nixon also approved wiretapping, as well as surveillance of many of his enemies.

As the election of 1972 drew nearer, Nixon became almost single-mindedly obsessed with winning reelection. He wanted to win by the largest margin in US history. So, he started a committee for reelection. The Committee to Re-elect the President was given $500,000 in campaign funds, as well as permission to do whatever was necessary to get him reelected.

On this committee were lawyer G. Gordon Liddy and intelligence officer Howard Hunt. By all accounts, Liddy was the mastermind behind the future scandal, and it was his idea to break into the Democratic National Committee (DNC) headquarters on the sixth floor of an office building in the Watergate complex. He and Hunt hired five Cuban American CIA officers to do their dirty work. On May 28, 1972, Bernard Barker, Virgilio Gonzalez, Eugenio Martínez, James W. McCord Jr., and Frank Sturgis broke into the Watergate complex and bugged two office phones. What were they hoping to find? Information and campaign strategies of the Democratic Party, specifically Senator George McGovern from South Dakota, who was Nixon's primary rival in the election, and DNC chairman Larry O'Brien. The caper went off without a hitch. The five men left the complex without discovery, while Liddy and Hunt stayed in a hotel room in Watergate. Former FBI agent Alfred Baldwin was given the task of listening to anything recorded by the wiretapping and reporting it back to Hunt. For twenty days, he did just that, collecting snippets of office gossip. But he collected no insight into the DNC campaign or Senator McGovern. And that's when he discovered that one of the bugs was malfunctioning.

On June 17, the five men were collected once again to break into the DNC headquarters and fix the bug. Liddy and Hunt were once again stationed in the hotel to monitor progress. Baldwin served as a lookout from the Howard Johnson hotel across the street. The five burglars got into the office easily, taping the latch on the door so it could easily be opened and closed. This was a technique used by the cleaning crew at Watergate. But around 1 a.m., security guard Frank Wills noticed the tape on the stairwell door. What the burglars and their bosses didn't know, but Frank Wills did, was that the cleaning crew had already finished for the night. Suspicious, Wills called the police.

Across the street, Baldwin noticed three men pull up outside the Watergate office building in an unmarked car. They were dressed in plain clothes. At first, Baldwin didn't see anything out of the ordinary occurring. Until a light went on in the building. He tried to contact the five men inside the building, or Hunt and Liddy, but was unable to. The three men were, in fact, plainclothes police officers who arrested Bernard Barker, Virgilio Gonzalez, Eugenio Martínez, James W. McCord Jr., and Frank Sturgis at gunpoint.

When the FBI was handed the investigation, it was discovered that James McGovern was the chief of security for the Committee to Re-elect the President. They also discovered Baldwin's hiding place in the Howard Johnson hotel, and discovered two address books, as well as a check signed by Howard Hunt. And that's when the pieces started falling into place.

On July 10, 1972, Alfred Baldwin approached the FBI to tell them his story. He said he had tried to contact Hunt or Liddy, but had never been given further instructions. He agreed to testify about the criminal activity surrounding the break-in at Watergate, in exchange for immunity. In September, a federal grand jury indicted the five burglars along with G. Gordon Liddy and Howard Hunt. All seven men except Liddy and McGovern pleaded guilty to charges of burglary, wiretapping, and conspiracy.

Initially, there was no evidence that the White House had any knowledge of the wiretapping or break-in. In fact, a recording from the Oval Office at the time reveals Nixon asking: "Who is the a**hole who ordered it?" Publicly, the president seemed skeptical about the break-in, calling it a "third rate burglary attempt." But privately, Nixon asked his chief of staff, H. R. Haldeman, to have the CIA block the FBI's investigation into who had funded the burglars.

As the case was drawn out in court, reporter Bob Woodward received a phone call from a high-ranking official in the White House, who wished to remain anonymous. Woodward met this source in a parking garage in Washington, DC. Known only as "Deep Throat," this confidential informant told Woodward that there had been much surveillance done on the part of the White House into the lives of American citizens and politicians, as well as the fact that there was a lot of money secretly being moved around. Woodward broke the story the next day. And the news of Watergate government surveillance entered into the American consciousness.

Despite all of this, Nixon got his wish and was reelected in the largest landslide in US history in November 1972. His platform? To stop the war in Vietnam.

In January of 1973, the court case began against the Watergate conspirators (or the Watergate Seven, as the press began calling them). Every journalist in the nation was covering the story. And every American was watching. That same month, just after being officially declared president again, Nixon brought lawyer John Dean into his inner circle. Dean's job? To control the information coming out of the White House to the press. As the court case continued, all seven men were found guilty of conspiracy, burglary, and wiretapping. All were given prison sentences. But the most damning evidence was given by a letter written by James McGovern and read in open court. In it, he declared that "there was political pressure placed on the defendants to plead guilty and remain silent." The letter also implicated several high-ranking officials in the Nixon administration, including John Dean and Attorney General John N. Mitchell. That was when the investigation reached a breaking point. Did the White House, specifically the president of the United States, have any knowledge of the break in at the DNC? Who was paying the legal bills for the burglars? What kind of campaign had the president run in order to get reelected?

On February 7, 1973, the US Senate voted 77-0 to establish a committee dedicated to investigating Watergate. Nixon was clearly feeling the pressure from outside. His staff noticed that he was becoming increasingly paranoid and moody.

In April, Nixon felt a need to distance himself from the rapidly growing scandal. He forced his chief of staff, H. R. Haldeman, and political aide John Ehrlichman to resign from their posts. He fired White House counsel John Dean. In a public speech, he told the American people it was possible that his staff had something to do with Watergat and that was why a new administration must be formed. He had hoped that would be the end of the scandal. But it wasn't.

The Watergate hearings were broadcast on television from May 17 to August 7, 1973. Every newspaper and television station in the country sent journalists to DC to report about the hearings. The scandal was heating up, and the American public wanted the truth. Had they re-elected a crook?

As the hearings continued, many White House staffers, including John Dean, were called to testify. On June 28, John Dean testified before the committee for eight hours, releasing a 245 page document on what had occurred at the White

House under Nixon's eye. He claimed there had been many discussions about the Watergate scandal and how best to inhibit the FBI's investigation into the matter.

But on Friday, July 13, 1973, the most damning piece of evidence came to light. White House assistant Andrew Butterfield was asked by deputy minority counsel Donald Sanders if there was any sort of recording going on in the Oval Office. Butterfield was hesitant to answer, but finally, he answered with a resounding yes. Dean echoed this news, stating that he often felt as though he was being recorded in the Oval Office during private meetings with the president and his aides. This was a bombshell. The president had been recording everything that happened in the Oval Office. While the White House had been filled with recording devices since the administration of Franklin Roosevelt, Nixon, it turned out, had the most extensive recording system to date. Nixon later claimed he had recorded everything for posterity, so that he could write a memoir one day. Even if this wasn't the case, the tapes were the personal property of Nixon, not the White House or the government. Immediately, Nixon was subpoenaed for the tapes, but he refused, citing executive privilege. He ordered the subpoena to be dropped. But it wasn't.

On October 20, 1974, Nixon tried to force the new attorney general, Elliot Richardson, and deputy William Ruckelshaus to fire special prosecutor Archibald Cox, who had subpoenaed the tapes. In protest, the two men resigned. Nixon continued desperately searching within the Justice Department for someone to do his dirty work. Finally, Solicitor General Robert Bork agreed and fired Cox. These actions, dubbed the "Saturday Night Massacre" by the media, were highly criticized and spurred Nixon to give his most famous address to the American people. "I am not a crook," he swore to the press. But no one quite believed him.

In April of 1974, Nixon finally released edited transcripts

of the tapes. And in July, the tapes were finally released. The hours and hours of recordings were listened to by the committee. One recording revealed that Nixon had approved paying the men who broke in to the DNC, as well as offering more and more money (from campaign funds) for their silence, as well as their legal bills. But as damning as that was, it was what *wasn't* on the tapes that intrigued investigators. Several tapes had missing segments, which, it was clear, held even worse offenses by the president. His personal secretary, Rose Mary Woods, claimed she accidentally erased the tapes while transcribing them. But no one believed her, especially since it was proved she claimed several sections had been erased multiple times.

On July 27, 1974, the House Judiciary Committee voted 27–11 to recommend the first article of impeachment against the president: obstruction of justice. The second article, abuse of power, was recommended two days later. The third article, contempt of Congress was recommended the following day.

But the "smoking gun" came on August 5, 1974. In a recording from June 23, 1972, Nixon asked then chief of staff Haldeman to interfere with the FBI's investigation into Watergate. There was no refuting it now: Nixon and his staff had planned, executed, and paid for the break-in of the DNC. And then had spent the next two years covering it up. Not only had Nixon had knowledge of the break-in from the beginning, he had been involved in covering it up. It turned out Nixon was, indeed, a crook.

But the story doesn't end there. Nixon was still president, albeit a despised one. The eleven senators who had opposed impeaching the president were now on board. There was no doubt. The Justice Department, the White House, and the American people no longer wanted Richard Millhouse Nixon as their president. In order to avoid an ugly public impeachment trial, Nixon resigned. In an address to the American public on August 7, 1974, Nixon stated:

*I have never been a quitter. To leave office before my term is completed is abhorrent to every instinct in my body. But as President, I must put the interest of America first. America needs a full-time President and a full-time Congress, particularly at this time with problems we face at home and abroad. To continue to fight through the months ahead for my personal vindication would almost totally absorb the time and attention of both the President and the Congress in a period when our entire focus should be on the great issues of peace abroad and prosperity without inflation at home. Therefore, I shall resign the Presidency effective at noon tomorrow. Vice President Ford will be sworn in as President at that hour in this office.*

Congress dropped their impeachment proceedings against Nixon after he resigned. Former vice president Gerald Ford followed Nixon in the Oval Office. A month later, the president issued a pardon for Nixon, stating that it was in the best interest of the American people. Nixon's situation was "an American tragedy in which we all have played a part. It could go on and on and on, or someone must write the end to it. I have concluded that only I can do that, and if I can, I must." Political analysts posit that this led to the election of Jimmy Carter, a Democrat whose platform was honesty in government, in 1976. The American people were disgusted by the actions that the Republican Party had committed, covered up, and pardoned.

As a result of the Watergate scandal, Congress passed several laws to prevent such an occurrence from happening again. Congress cut postwar funding in Vietnam, which directly led to the fall of Saigon and marked the end of the Vietnam War. Congress also passed the War Powers Act, which restricted the president's ability to enter a prolonged military conflict. But possibly the most influential piece of legislation passed by Congress at the time stated that all candidates for public office must disclose information about campaign funds, includ-

President Richard Nixon addressed the Watergate scandal during a TV address to the nation in 1973.

ing how it was raised and how it was used.

In 1994, Richard Nixon died at the age of eighty-one. He maintained his innocence for the rest of his life, though few believed him. In 1978, he released the memoir  for which he had been recording his Oval Office meetings. It was a best seller, in part because the American people were hoping for a confession that they never got. He spent the rest of his life giving lectures and making public appearances. He was not given a full state funeral, but it was nonetheless a politically charged affair. Five presints attended the funeral, and an estimated forty-two thousand mourners lined up to pay their respects.

In May of 2005, "Deep Throat" was finally revealed as Mark Felt, the former assistant director of the FBI. He had been snubbed by Nixon (who had suspected him of being a leak) for the position of director of the FBI after the death of J. Edgar Hoover. More important, though, Felt knew that the public needed to know about Nixon's "dirty tricks" campaign.

No matter the political and personal opinions of President Richard Nixon, one thing is certain: he changed the American political system, as well as the role of the president in the public eye. Nixon ended any idea that the president was above reproach, and that he (or she) was a figure that embodied moral perfection. Richard Nixon went down in history as a man embroiled in a scandal of his own making, who forever changed the political game of an entire nation and the way campaigning for public office is conducted. It can be said that our very long and public elections for political office are a direct result of Nixon and the Watergate scandal. Even the term "Watergate", or more specifically the suffix "-gate" have become synonymous with political scandals in the United States. But what even Nixon didn't know during the time was that his actions would encompass political scandal on a much grander scale. No political scandal has ever quite matched Watergate. No president has divided a nation so strongly. And no president likely will ever have the same effect on the American conscious.

## Benghazi

On the night of September 11, 2012, the city of Benghazi, Libya, erupted in violence. Islamic militants attacked a diplomatic compound, which housed the US consulate, along with many other military and political figures. US Ambassador J. Christopher Stevens and Foreign Service information management officer Sean Smith were killed as their building was lit on fire using diesel fuel to stoke the flames. It is most likely the two men died from smoke inhalation.

An hour later, there was a second assault on a CIA annex about a mile away. Two CIA contractors and former Navy

SEALs Tyrone S. Woods and Glen Doherty were killed. Ten others were injured in what has come to be called the "Battle of Benghazi."

The next day, President Barack Obama and Secretary of State Hillary Clinton told the US media that the attack was spontaneous, a protest in response to a video released on YouTube called *Innocence of Muslims*, which depicts the prophet Mohammed, considered blasphemy in the religion of Islam. But many didn't believe the government's assessment of the situation. Why were four American officials killed in Benghazi? Could it have been prevented?

Libya was a place of political turmoil. It had been through revolution the year before, overthrowing dictator Muammar Gaddafi. Rebel forces, along with the Libyan military and help from the United Nations and US military forces, had overthrown the dictator and brought about a revolution. But soon, rebel forces began to turn against each other, leaving Libya, Syria, and many other areas in the Middle East in turmoil.

But on September 12, 2012, the day after the attacks, protesters in Benghazi and Tripoli condemned the actions of the attackers, who, it was determined, were not part of the official military. According to a Gallup poll, 52 percent of Libyans had respected Ambassador Stevens. Libyan officials suggested the attack had been prompted by loyalists of Gaddafi. But was this all there was to the story? A lone attack in response to a revolution?

Immediately after the attacks, the US increased security at diplomatic and military posts worldwide. Just a few days after the attacks, an investigation by US officials, the FBI, and the CIA began. And that was when it was realized there were more questions than answers about the Battle of Benghazi.

By reviewing official requests from agents on the ground, it was determined that there had been multiple requests for increased security. There had been twenty security instances in the month of August alone. CIA agents on the ground had created a briefing about the many terrorist organizations in the area. It was determined that while the Benghazi attacks were not conducted by al-Qaeda, whic was the United States' largest Islamic terrorist enemy at the time, it was clear that Islamic extremist terrorist militants had been behind the attack. (ISIS would not fully emerge in Libya for another two years).

A full-scale investigation was launched, including an official report released in 2013. This report by the Senate determined that the attack had, in fact, been preventable. The State Department had, quite simply, not responded quickly enough to requests for more security. Ambassador Stevens had told his colleagues and executives in Washington about the potentially volatile situation in Benghazi. It was determined that the attacks were opportunistic, not a protest, and that, in truth, these attacks were a direct show of force against American occupation in Libya.

Hillary Clinton was particularly under fire from Congress and the media. It seemed that her emails had not all been sent via a secure government server and that she might have ignored advice from agents on the ground in Benghazi, including Ambassador Stevens. According to the 2013 report, the White House had hampered the FBI investigation into the attack, and the State Department didn't provide all the information needed to prevent the attack or to tell the truth of the situation in Benghazi. In 2016, Clinton sat through an eleven-and-a-half-hour Congressional interrogation to determine whether she had had prior intelligence of a potential attack and had simply ignored it. It was determined that Clinton had been receiving contradictory information, and she herself had no personal part to play in preventing the attacks. Like many other politicians and officials in the State Department, Clinton said the attacks were regrettable, and they wanted to determine how the deaths of four Americans had occurred.

Many speculate that the military, and more specifically the State Department and the White House, have been hiding the truth about the Benghazi attacks and that there is more to learn about that night. And while inquiries are still being made and the FBI and CIA are still probing into emails, personal correspondences, and many other forms of communication between forces on the ground and leaders in Washington, the truth is that while the State Department and the White House may have downplayed the attack at first, and while the loss of life may have been preventable, the attacks in Benghazi in September 2012 were the direct result of an unstable political situation in a nation riddled with violence.

Since these attacks, the situation in Libya and surrounding countries has gotten no better. ISIS has emerged to take control of the country, displacing hundreds of thousands from their homes and creating a worldwide refugee crisis. ISIS is destroying ancient cities and landmarks and killing thousands of soldiers. In truth, Benghazi was the beginning of a larger, more volatile situation in the Middle East, an area that has never truly seen peace. And it appears as though peace is not on the horizon, no matter what intelligence is spread or not.

# CHAPTER THREE: SECRETS OF THE HEART

## THE KING AND MRS. SIMPSON

Edward, Prince of Wales, kept a secret close to his heart for months. He had fallen desperately in love with a woman that his position as king would never allow him to marry. And yet, hopelessly and obsessively, he could not end the affair. Eventually, he abandoned his throne in order to stay with American divorcée Wallis Simpson. But for the British people, the prince's love affair was kept secret. While abroad people snickered over the weak Edward's hopeless devotion for Simpson, censors and the British establishment worked hard to keep the British people in the dark about their King's lover. It was a calculated move designed to keep an entire nation cut off from reality. It was hardly surprising, therefore, that once the secret was out, it engulfed Edward, Wallis, the establishment, and the royal family like a tidal wave.

Edward VIII was king of Great Britain for 326 days before he abdicated his throne for the woman he loved. He had been blindly in love with Wallis Simpson for nearly three years. The object of His Majesty's desire was the lady who he had met in 1931, a witty but rather plain thirty-four-year-old twice divorced American socialite, who had had a childhood and upbringing just about as far as one could get from the House of Windsor. Her father, a businessman from Maryland, had died when she was just five months old, and she had been raised in Baltimore by her mother. She married a Navy pilot in 1916, confessing that she found the combination of uniform and heroic courage a thrilling combination. But her union with Earl Winfield Spencer was short lived and they were separated in 1922. Her second marriage came in 1928 to Ernest Simpson, a half British and half American businessman, who was head of his family's shipping company in London. It was his arrival in Britain in 1929 that thrust Wallis Simpson onto the London social scene. It had always been an ambition of her mother's that and Wallis should elevate herself within society, leaving behind the low social order and poverty of her upbringing. With her marriage to Ernest she seemed to have accomplished that goal and established a reputation among the rich and privileged as something of an amusing and competent hostess. She moved among diplomats, lords and ladies, and celebrities—and loved it. However as Wallis began to enjoy the London social scene more and more, she began to find her husband staid, dull, and uninteresting.

In December 1930, the new first secretary at the American Embassy, Benjamin Thaw, was invited to dinner at the Simpsons. He came with his wife, Consuelo, and her sister Thelma, Viscountess Furness. Lady Furness, a vampish beauty with affected Hollywood starlet looks and manners, had her own secret—she was mistress to Edward, the prince of Wales. A friendship burgeoned between the three women, with Thelma confiding to Wallis about her secret love. Eventually, the Simpsons dined with the prince and were soon regular visitors to his country retreat. He also dined at the Simpsons' flat off Oxford Street. In January 1934 the viscountess, at a dinner party, discreetly said to Wallis Simpson: "I am making a trip to the United States. Please would you look after the Prince to make sure he isn't lonely?" Wallis looked after him all right, rather a little too well for Thelma's liking. By the time she returned in the spring, Wallis and the Prince were lovers.

The secret of the relationship was shared by a small elite group. In the 1930s the press was far more conservative and did not employ professional "royal watchers" as it does today. Conversely, Edward was being sucked into an emotional vortex that would run directly contrary to his responsibilities as the future king of Great Britain. The secret love letters, which were released after Wallis Simpson's death at the age of eighty-nine in 1986, showed the bizarre mother-son relationship that the couple shared, despite the fact that Wallis was two years younger than the prince. His letters are full of infantile pleading, a need to be reassured, indulged, and protected, adoring in his affections for her. Hers are admonishing, stern, sensible, and even possessive.

The privileged group of friends who in the early days witnessed them together say that he was completely captivated by her. She was slender, sophisticated, poised, elegant, and witty and the exact opposite of the rather boyish would-be king of Great Britain.

It is not known at which exact date the prince told the royal family of his love for Wallis Simpson. But they could well have learned from the prince's indiscreet flaunting of his new mistress on trips to Paris, the French Riviera, Budapest, Berlin, and Italy. The foreign press had a field day. Detailed accounts of their trysts in romantic hotels were published in every language from French to Finnish and even the United States press got in on the act, calling Wallis "Queen Wally."

Amazingly, Fleet Street, where the British press was housed, didn't print a single word about the affair. The newspapers then were owned by the powerful press barons, who saw it as their duty to preserve the facade of the royal family, even if their future king was behaving like a playboy. Newspapers coming into the country from overseas which had references to the liaison were removed before the British public could glean knowledge of the affair betpeen their prince and a twice-divorced American socialite. The US press in particular went to town with photographs and stories about the couple's visits to Yugoslavia, Greece, and Turkey.

Prince Edward became King Edward VIII in December 1935. The affair was at its height and the love letters from Edward to Wallis became ever more sloppy and infantile. But Edward still had the British establishment on his side—an institution capable of handling so much indiscretion just as long as it is discreet. But the turning point occurred on December 3, 1936. Some weeks before, Wallis had finally received a divorce from her husband. Prime Minister Stanley Baldwin, who knew then of the entanglement between Edward and Wallis, asked the king to persuade Wallis not to go through with the divorce. But Edward told him, "I have no right to interfere with the affairs of an individual. It would be wrong were I to attempt to influence Mrs. Simpson just because she happens to be a friend of the king." Secretly, it was what he had wished and conspired for. In six months time, before his coronation, he would be free to wed her.

The conspiracy of silence ended when the Bishop of Bradford, Dr. Blunt, publicly chastised Edward for his carefree lifestyle, which he said was incongruous with a man who was the head of the British Empire. The newspapers construed that the Bishop's outburst was aimed directly at the relationship between the King and Wallis Simpson. The secret was out. Edward was swamped by the public reaction to his affair and naively believed that the establishment and the people would understand his affair of the heart. But there would be no sympathetic tears shed for his blighted love. Queen Mary, his mother, was outraged and sent for Baldwin at Buckingham Palace. Edward had hoped to move Baldwin into accepting Wallis as his bride and the future Queen of England. Edward had not yet had his coronation and he believed his popularity with the British people would win through and he would be allowed to marry Wallis. Baldwin told him flatly, "We will not have it sir. People are talking about you and this American woman. I have had so many nasty letters from people who respected your father and who do not appreciate the way you are going on."

In the eight days between revelation and King Edward's abdication, Wallis was subjected to a terrible hate campaign. Rocks were hurled through the window of her London home and she received threatening and hurtful letters. Children sang in the streets: "Hark the Herald Angels Sing, Mrs Simpson's pinched our King." Wallis fled to the south of France while Edward battled against the established order and his own feelings. He was told to ditch Wallis and to assume the responsibilities to which his whole life had been leading, like a man. He tried to sway various influential politicians and press barons, but without much success. He found an ally in Winston Churchill who, at a lunch with playwright Noel Coward, remarked: "Why shouldn't the king marry his cutie?" "Because," remarked Coward, "England does not want a Queen Cutie."

King Edward VII abdicated the English throne in order to pursue a life with Mrs. Wallis Simpson. The choice was either a scandal or a great love story, depending on one's opinion.

Finally Edward approached the publisher of the *Daily Mail*, Esmond Harmsworth, who suggested the idea of a morganatic marriage, once popular in German royal states, in which Wallis could become his bride, but would not assume the title of queen. Her children similarly would have no rights to the throne of Great Britain. Wallis begrudgingly accepted, but it was to no avail; the cabinet would not entertain the idea. If

Edward were to remain as king, it would be without Wallis Simpson at his side.

The king, hopelessly, blindly, and devotedly in love with Wallis, decided to abdicate his throne in order to resolve the constitutional crisis looming over Britain. When Wallis heard that he had stepped down from the throne on December 11, 1936, and broadcast his message to the British people the following night, she wept. Later in her memoirs she wrote: "I was lying on the sofa with my hands over my eyes, trying to hide my tears." The king had told the nation that he could not rule without the woman he loved by his side. Edward then left for France, never again to set foot on the shores of his beloved Great Britain.

The couple lived in a splendid white chateau on the outskirts of Paris. They married in the Loire Valley and remained as distant outcasts from the royal family until their deaths—he in May 1972, aged seventy-seven, and she fourteen years later.

Only at Edward's funeral at St George's Chapel, in Windsor, did Wallis come to see the members of the royal family that she had so wished to join. She spent one night in Buckingham Palace before returning to her exile in Paris. She ended her days lonely and bedridden, a sad figure whose secret affair burgeoned into one of the classic romantic tragedies of the century. On her dressing room table she kept a framed message penned by Edward, who assumed the title of duke of Windsor after his abdication. The touching lines read: "My friend, with thee to live alone, methinks were better than to own, a crown, a sceptre, and a throne."

## The President and Marilyn Monroe

For almost fifty years the FBI was ruled with an iron fist by J. Edgar Hoover, a man possessed by huge prejudice, intense paranoia, and an obsession with other people's sex lives. Hoover always looked for weaknesses in his real or imagined enemies, and built up files that gave him immense potential power over them. For years, his twisted brain consumed and collated information ready to be put to use. And no public figure had a bigger personal file within Hoover's office than the president of the United States of America, the charismatic John F. Kennedy.

Kennedy seemed to embody the opposite of the things which Hoover believed were right. Always hunting communists and liberals, Hoover despised the Kennedy reforms of the racist school system in the southern states and his links with civil rights leader Martin Luther King Jr. Hoover set out to discover the weaknesses of John F. Kennedy. He found them not in booze, or pornography, bribery, civic corruption, or money. Kennedy's weakness was sex.

He had many illicit affairs during his marriage to his wife Jacqueline, both before he stepped into the White House and after. However, unknown to Kennedy at the start of his tenure of office, Hoover had placed many key White House personnel on the FBI payroll as his personal spies within the president's official residence. Kennedy's telephone conversations were taped, his secret meetings with women were watched and time stamped. Kennedy's attraction to and for other women was something that revolted Hoover. But something that has remained a mystery to this day is whether Kennedy had an affair with the biggest sex symbol of the time—Marilyn Monroe. His brother Robert Kennedy was also widely rumored to have shared the bed of the Hollywood starlet, who allegedly killed herself with barbiturates in August 1962 at the age of thirty-six. Since her death, the ghost of Marilyn Monroe has never been laid to rest. Many theories have surfaced: stories that her death was not a suicide after all, but in fact a way for the government to cover up the illicit affairs from the American pubic.

Marilyn's affair with President Kennedy was said to have been known by all, but discussed by none. Although never

Both Robert Kennedy and his brother John are believed to have carried on affairs with actress and icon Marilyn Monroe. Rumors continue to swirl that they may have been behind her death.

publicly acknowledged, it was made fairly clear when she sang "Happy Birthday" to the president at his birthday celebration in Madison Square Garden in 1962, just three months before her death.

And her death, some allege, was brought about because she intended to publicly expose her affair with the president. There have been other bizarre theories. Did mobsters bug the star's bedroom in a bid to blackmail the Kennedys, who were cracking down hard on organized crime? Did Robert Kennedy, then US attorney general, break off his relationship with Marilyn on the very day she died? Did the Kennedys' brother-in-law, the actor Peter Lawford, destroy a suicide note from Marilyn that may have leaked the sensational news that she bedded the two most powerful men in the United States? Was she murdered in a move guaranteed to keep her silent? No serious investigation has ever been conducted into these allegations, but still the story won't die. Many theorize that the star's death had more to do with what she might have known about the politicians and leaders in the United States than with her love for two brothers.

The story of the enigmas of the Kennedy brothers and Marilyn Monroe has continued to fascinate conspiracy theorists, fans, and journalists alike. And the suspicious circumstances of her death have remained in the American consciousness, even over half a century after her death.

One of Lawford's ex-wives, Deborah Gould, said the affair with Jack Kennedy began before he took office in 1961. He broke it off, allegedly because he found Marilyn "dangerously talkative." Initially Bobby was just used as the messenger boy, says Gould, but then he found himself spellbound by her beauty and sensuousness. But Lawford, who died in 1984, repeatedly and vehemently denied that the affairs had ever taken place. His denial of the secret trysts is not believed by investigative journalist Anthony Summers who, in his book about Marilyn called *Goddess*, speculated:

> *It seems that for many months she engaged in intermittent sexual encounters with both the President and Robert Kennedy. For both the brothers and for Marilyn, there had been an initial attraction between stars, each glittering prizes in the interlocking galaxies of politics and show business. The Kennedy brothers, bred to the knowledge that they could have any woman they desired, at first failed to perceive that in Marilyn Monroe they were dealing with a woman who was doubly dangerous.*

Summers said that the nature of the danger lay in the fact that she represented a threat to both of their political lives. She was despondent over frequent miscarriages and abortions and her fading career. There were rumors that her grip on reality was ebbing away too. It was well known that the star was using many prescription drugs and seeing a psychiatrist. She had also been seen drunk in public, as well as disoriented and depressed.

On the night Marilyn died, Summers speculates that Peter Lawford, who was the last person to speak to her on the telephone, came to Marilyn's house before she was dead and, possibly with Robert Kennedy, took the dying actress to a hospital in Santa Monica. However, when Monroe died, the corpse was rushed back to her home and the death scene was staged before the police were called. His book makes no firm charge, but leaves open the possibility that "someone else administered the fatal overdose." Lynn Franklin, a retired LAPD officer seems to back this story. Despite a very public showing in northern California with his family all weekend, Franklin claims he saw Bobby Kennedy in LA that night. Franklin states that he had pulled over a black sedan for speeding. Inside were Bobby Kennedy and his brother-in-law Peter Lawford driving. In the backseat, Franklin says, was Marilyn's psychiatrist, Dr. Greenson.

Milo Speriglio, head of a private detective agency in Los Angeles, has been fascinated with Marilyn Monroe, her apparent liaison with the Kennedys, and her untimely death ever since she was found in the early morning of August 5, 1962. He is convinced she was murdered.

Speriglio began with a reinvestigation of the inquest and police reports. The coroner ruled suicide after hearing that she had swallowed forty-seven capsules of barbiturates. But the autopsy stated that the stomach was almost completely empty except for a small residue of brownish liquid. Also, no water was found in her stomach. Did she take forty-seven pills without any water? Sergeant Jack Clemmons, the police officer first at the scene in her home in the LA suburb of Brentwood, noticed that there was no vomit around—usually the first sign that someone has tried suicide with pills—no glass, no water. Jack Clemmons left the force and told Speriglio he had recommended an investigation to his superiors. But he was told to totally forget about the idea.

The autopsy was also incomplete. Although all the proper tissue samples were taken from Monroe's body, only the liver and blood were tested, proving she did, indeed, have a lethal dose of barbiturates and alcohol in her system. Discoloration on the skin suggested the body had been moved after death, perhaps more than once. There was no suicide note ever found on the scene or anywhere in Monroe's Brentwood home. Former LA Deputy DA John Minor, who was the liaison between the coroner's office and the police department claimed: "I should've called for a criminal investigation. But most all the evidence had been destroyed. Removed!"

Speriglio tried to get copies of Marilyn's phone bills, since she was known to have been on the phone hours before her death, and perhaps even at time of her death, since the phone's receiver was found in her hand, but they had apparently gone "missing." He tried to find the diary that had been passed into the custody of deputy coroner's aide Lionel Grandison, who signed Marilyn's death certificate. Speriglio claimed Grandison told him he had looked through the book and seen references to the Kennedys and some Mafia figures in San Diego. But when Speriglio returned with a request to see the diary, the book was not only gone but had also been struck from the inventory of personal effects turned over to the state.

The private eye also says he had evidence that the Monroe's home was bugged—one of his sources was Bernard Spindel, an expert wiretapper who was arrested by the FBI in 1966 and who died in prison before Speriglio could get his hands on the tapes he possessed. But before he died, he filed a petition to the Supreme Court citing return of "a confidential file containing tapes and evidence concerning circumstances surrounding the death of Marilyn Monroe which strongly suggests the official reported circumstances of her demise are erroneous." Speriglio believed from talking to other informants in the Senate that Marilyn was preparing a news conference to get back at the Kennedys—spilling the beans not only on their love affairs, but the death plots which Kennedy had told her about and which were aimed at Cuban dictator Fidel Castro and many other state secrets.

This would have been a terrible blow to Hoover, who had kept an eye on Marilyn since her marriage to Arthur Miller, a famous playwright who was also a card-carrying member of the Communist Party. Not only would America's sweetheart lay waste to the morality and upstanding positions of the president and the attorney general of the United States, but would also destroy many state secrets in the process. A report from August 2, just two days before her death, states there was a CIA surveillance on her home.

Given this evidence, there is a possibility that the CIA was involved in Marilyn's death; plotters in the bizarre power-play who may have administered a lethal injection of barbiturates to prevent a scandal from engulfing the White House. Speriglio said: "In 1980 under the Freedom of Information Act, I petitioned the FBI for Marilyn Monroe's file. Most of the material was blanked out and, under orders of then FBI director William Webster, eighteen of the forty-three pages were completely withheld. The reason given for the exempted eighteen pages was national defense and foreign policy." The remaining material was apparently useless and shed no light on the death of the famous film star.

Did Marilyn Monroe know secrets about the most influential political dynasty in the United States? Had the brothers told her secrets about foreign affairs as a form of pillow talk? Or had she ever even had an affair with either (or both) of them at all? Was the death of the beloved film star, troubled and depressed, really a suicide? Or was it some masterful cover-up to keep her quiet? We may never know the answers to these questions. Sadly both John F. Kennedy and his brother were assassinated, taking with them to their graves the truth about their relationship with Marilyn Monroe. She led a troubled life, desperate for the love and attention she never received as a child. Her death was indeed a tragedy, no matter if she committed suicide or if she was murdered. But one thing is certain: Marilyn Monroe will forever be linked to President John F. Kennedy, his brother Robert, and what can happen behind closed doors in a celebrity's life.

## Woody Allen's Unconventional Family

Woody Allen is one of Hollywood's greatest gems. He is a filmmaker, actor, screenwriter, playwright, musician, and comedian responsible for entertaining audiences for more than six decades. Some of his works include *Annie Hall* (1977), *Manhattan* (1979), *Bullets Over Broadway* (1994), and more recently, *Match Point* (2005), *Vicky Cristina Barcelona* (2008), *Midnight in Paris* (2011), *Blue Jasmine* (2013), and *Irrational Man* (2015). He has consistently produced, starred in, directed, or written at least one film every year since 1965—an incredible feat. He has worked with some of the best actors in the world both onscreen and onstage, and many consider it to be an honor to work with him.

But Woody Allen's personal life is... unconventional, to say the least. Around 1980, Allen met the beautiful actress Mia Farrow, who lived not far from Allen and had adopted several children. Allen had been married twice before and had a relationship with costar Diane Keaton and with Stacey Nelkin, who was seventeen when the two met. But after meeting, Allen and Farrow were nearly inseparable. After two years together, Allen and Farrow adopted two children in 1991: Dylan ( also known as Eliza) and Moeshe (known as Moses). The couple never officially married or moved in together, but Allen saw his children every day. The couple also had a biological child together, Satchel Farrow (known as Ronan).

But just a couple of months later, Farrow discovered nude photos of her daughter, Soon-Yi Previn, in Allen's apartment. (Farrow had adopted the girl from Korea with her former husband, Andre Previn.) Soon-Yi Previn was twenty-one years old by this time, but the photos were a shock to Farrow. When she confronted Allen, the filmmaker admitted he was having an affair with Farrow's daughter. The couple had a bitter breakup that resulted in custody battles, and Soon-Yi moved in with Allen. The two were married five years later.

To make things even stranger, Farrow claimed in 2013 that Allen's son Ronan might actually be the biological child of Frank Sinatra, her first husband, with whom she "never really broke up." There were also allegations that Allen had molested his daughter, Dylan, for which Allen was thoroughly investigated. He was even under treatment with a child psychologist for alleged inappropriate behavior with his daughter. Although Farrow began a lengthy court case, the courts declined to press charges in order to protect the "child victim." Farrow unsuccessfully attempted to have her adoptions with Allen nullified legally, and Allen continues to be their legal father. He has also adopted two daughters with Soon-Yi.

## James McGreevey

James McGreevey was a well-liked politician. The governor of New Jersey was a Democrat and a champion for education and public policy. He welcomed immigrants and all nationalities into his home state. He was married with two children and had attended some of the United States' most prestigious universities, including Columbia, Georgetown, and Harvard. He was charming, charismatic, and well-loved by his constituents. But James McGreevey had a secret. He was gay.

In 2001, his second time running for governor of New Jersey, McGreevey won with 56 percent of the vote. He inherited a $5 million budget deficit. To counteract this, McGreevey raised the tax on cigarettes and also gave the wealthy a tax increase. He implemented stem-cell research in New Jersey in order to find cures for diseases such as cancer, multiple sclerosis, and AIDS. He also took a pro-choice stance on abortion and signed a law in 2004 giving same-sex couples domestic partnership status.

Not long after becoming governor, McGreevey had the opportunity to appoint a new homeland security advisor. He chose Golan Cipel, an Israeli-born former military man who had served in the Israel Defense Forces (IDF) for five years as a naval officer. McGreevey's appointment of Cipel was highly criticized. Cipel was not an American citizen, and, therefore, couldn't be given a very high level of security clearance. And on top of that, there were rumors about the two men's relationship. According to reports, Cipel was a sailor and a poet who had struck up a "close relationship" with McGreevey. The two were known to travel together. Rumors flew about the nature of McGreevey's relationship with Cipel. In 2002, Cipel stepped down from his position at McGreevey's request.

But the story doesn't end there. Cipel was angry with McGreevey for his treatment in the public eye. It is unclear whether or not the two had maintained their romantic relationship, but Cipel filed a sexual harassment suit against McGreevey in 2004. When news of the story broke, the press plagued McGreevey and his family with questions about his sexual orientation and his abilities to make rational decisions concerning government when he had clearly allowed his heart to guide him in his appointment of a high-ranking official.

New Jersey governor Jim McGreevey had disgraced wife Dina at his side when he resigned from his position.

At a press conference on August 12, 2004, with his wife Dina Matos at his side, McGreevey stunned the audience with his admission: "My truth is that I am a gay American." He also stated that he had engaged in an illicit but consensual affair with another man (aides later told the press is was Cipel). He resigned from office, effective in November. But his admission made him the first openly gay governor in US history.

Since then, McGreevey has published a memoir, aptly titled *The Confession*, about his public life in politics and his private life in the closet. In it, he described the duality of his life:

> *As glorious and meaningful as it would have been to have a loving and sound sexual experience with another man, I knew I'd have to undo my happiness step by step as I began chasing my dream of a public career and the kind of "acceptable" life*

*that went with it. So, instead, I settled for the detached anonymity of bookstores and rest stops—a compromise, but one that was wholly unfulfilling and morally unsatisfactory."*

After politics, McGreevey found a new calling: he went back to school, attending the General Theological Seminary, where he received the degree of daster of divinity. Although he has no parish, he is an Episcopal priest who volunteers for the Church of the Living Hope in Harlem, New York, where he helps former prisoners who are seeking rehabilitation and assistance acclimating to the world outside of prison walls.

It is clear that McGreevey seeks a life of public service and has found a new way to fulfill this. Striking balance in a very public life can be trying, and McGreevey, it seems, would rather keep his private life private now. Although he wrote a memoir and was the subject of a 2013 documentary entitled *Fall to Grace*, it is clear McGreevey, just like many of us, is grappling with how to become the best version of himself.

## The Lewinsky Scandal

When Monica Lewinsky confided to her friend Linda Tripp about the married man she was in love with, she had no idea that her phone calls were being recorded. Furthermore, she had no idea that those tapes would be released to the media, and nearly cost that married man— President Bill Clinton— his career.

Halfway through President Clinton's first term in the White House, twenty-one-year-old Monica Lewinsky became an intern there. Lewinsky described her personal interactions with the president as flirtatious at first. But the flirtation soon became much, much more. She described sneaking in and out of the Oval Office to see him, as well as the nature of their relationship as "messing around." But as the president hit the campaign trail for reelection, Lewinsky was left alone in

Washington, young, naive, and hopelessly in love with a very publicly married man.

On January 17, 1998, reporter Michael Isikoff broke the news to the nation that President Bill Clinton had been having an affair with a twenty-two-year-old White House intern. The *Washington Post* released another story just three days later. And a media frenzy ensued. Clinton vehemently denied the affair, but the media would not relent. In an address to the American people on January 26, 1998, Clinton famously stated: "I did not have sexual relations with that woman." But was it true?

For months, the media debated whether or not the affair had taken place. Some said the president was guilty of lying to the American people and obstruction of justice. Others stated that it was just the word of a lonely girl infatuated with the president.

But on July 28, 1998, a grand jury offered Lewinsky immunity in exchange for her testimony at a grand jury hearing. Former friend Linda Tripp had encouraged Lewinsky to save a blue dress that she had worn during a tryst with the president. That blue dress, along with the secretly recorded phone calls, gave evidence to the only possible conclusion: President Bill Clinton, had in fact had "sexual relations" with Monica Lewinsky.

On August 17, 1998, in a grand jury testimony, President Clinton admitted that he had an "improper physical relationship" with Monica Lewinsky. Although he knew it was scandalous, he seemed fairly certain in public appearances that the affair could be placed behind him, once the truth was out. He was so very wrong.

Presidential opposition was high in the Republicanamajority Congress. Many in Washington felt that the president had committed the crimes of obstruction of justice and perjury. Both of which are impeachable offenses. The House of Representative issued articles of impeachment against President Bill Clinton. But in a very close vote, President Clinton was acquitted, therefore able to stay in the White House as president of the United States.

After the Lewinsky scandal broke, newspapers around the country jumped to publish the salacious details of the president's affair.

The scandal led to pop-culture status for Lewinsky. Her immunity agreement stated that there were only certain things she could talk about in regards to the president and their affair. But she released a book with author Andrew Morton in 1999 called *Monica's Story*. She gave a famous, candid interview with Barbara Walters for ABC's *20/20* that same year. That interview was watched by seventy million Americans, a record-breaking audience for the news program. Lewinsky started a line of handbags and accessories and also received many endorsements, including with the dieting company Jenny Craig. She moved to Manhattan and became an A-list celebrity on the social scene. She made numerous television appearances, including on *Saturday Night Live!*, as well as *The View* and *Late Night with Jimmy Kimmel.*

But public life in the United States proved too much for Lewinsky, and she moved to London and earned a master's degree in social science. Nearly a decade later, Lewinsky wrote an article for *Vanity Fair* magazine entitled "Shame and Survival."In it she maintained that her relationship with the president was mutual, despite what he has continued to claim. And she candidly discussed what her life had become since having an affair with the president. She hadn't been able to get a job because of her notoriety. She is still considered "that woman" who almost took down a president with her illicit sexual prowess. It was so well received the magazine took her on as a contributor.

In 2014, Monica Lewinsky used her status as a publicly mocked individual to speak out against cyberbullying, calling herself "patient zero" in such instances. She even gave a TED talk in 2015, pleading for a more compassionate internet and media.

Bill Clinton has spent his time since the White House working with charity. The Clinton Foundation, founded in 2013 by Bill, his wife, Hillary, and his daughter, Chelsea, works to "strengthen the capacity of people throughout the world to meet the challenges of global interdependence."

The Lewinsky affair is a true case of "he said, she said." Lewinsky still maintains that her relationship with the president was mutual. In Clinton's 2004 biography *My Life*, he continued to claim that he didn't initiate anything and that he was a victim of circumstance and opportunity instigated by a sexually charged intern. We may never really know. What we do know is that the scandal created such a political frenzy it almost cost a man his presidency for something not at all related to affairs of state.

# CHAPTER FOUR: MILITARY SECRETS

## THE CAPTURE OF OSAMA BIN LADEN

On September 11, 2001, four passenger airliners were hijacked by al-Qaeda terrorists and crashed into both towers of the World Trade Center in New York City and the Pentagon in Washington, DC. The fourth plane crashed in Pennsylvania. In the events, 2, 996 people (including the hijackers) were killed and some 6,000 were injured. First responding firefighters and police also suffered major casualties. This event triggered massive changes in travel and homeland security and left a visible scar on the United States.

The United States immediately leapt to action to catch the men responsible. Al-Qaeda had claimed responsibility, but Osama bin Laden himself had not. However, he was known as the leader of the organization, and his capture became the number one priority of the US government. In December 2001, a few US troops with the aid of rebel forces on the ground bombarded the area of Tora Bora, where bin Laden was known to be hiding. The region is a vast cavernous system of caves and rough mountains. Despite the massive show of military force, bin Laden escaped into the wilderness of northern Pakistan unharmed.

Over the next decade, al-Qaeda continued to attack cities in the West. The United States and its allies continued surveillance of Afghanistan and Pakistan, searching for any sign of the leader of the most lethal terrorist organization in the world. Predator drones allowed for information to be collected without any physical threat to troops on the ground. Some video footage showed grainy images of a man who looked very much like bin Laden, but these were hard to verify, and did not give enough information to send in troops. Bin Laden became the world's most wanted man.

In 2003, the military shifted its focus to Saddam Hussein and a potential threat of nuclear weapons in Iraq (which would later be debunked). The media also shifted its focus away from the terrorist and onto the destruction of the dictator and the nation which he has held captive for decades. In 2004, bin Laden released another one of his videos to the public, openly taking responsibility for the attacks of September 11, 2001, and threatening American safety. And while these threats were taken seriously, there was no intelligence gathered on the organization or its leaders and where they might be.

But in 2008, President Barack Obama shifted the focus back onto Osama bin Laden, declaring that he was the number one enemy of the United States and that he must not only be stopped, but killed for the crimes he had committed and organized. In Guantánámo Bay, the US prison for international terrorists, al-Qaeda inmates suggested that there was a courier who should be investigated and watched more closely. This courier was the go-between for bin Laden and the rest of the world, distributing his messages, getting the leader supplies, and helping him stay in hiding.

And in March of 2011, the tip paid off when CIA intelligence officers followed this courier to a compound in Abbottabad, a prosperous town in Pakistan. This compound had high walls, and was known to house the number of people that intelligence officers assumed bin Laden had with him. Very few people ever came or went from this three-story house. They burned their own garbage and ran no electronics. It seemed an unlikely place for the world's worst terrorist to hide out. Not in the caves and mountains of Pakistan, but instead, in a wealthy suburb? President Obama gave the go-ahead to raid the compound.

On May 1, 2011, the Situation Room in the White House was filled with the president, his close staff, generals, and CIA and FBI officials. SEAL Team Six was deployed on the ground in Abbottabad, closing in on the compound. Three Black Hawk helicopters hovered over the area, trying to determine what sort of altercation might be awaiting inside.

As the SEALs invaded the compound, they immediately shot four people— al-Kuwati, bin Laden's courier, along with his wife and brother and one of bin Laden's sons were killed. A few moments later, the news was heard in the White House from the troops on the ground: "Geronimo is EKIA." Geronimo, the code name they had determined was appropriate for the terrorist leader, was an "enemy killed in action" at 1:25 a.m.

In an address to the American people, President Obama said: "Justice has been done." The terrorist responsible for the deaths of thousands of innocent people had finally been brought down.

Osama bin Laden was buried at sea on May 2, 2011, so that his grave could not become the sight of pilgrimages for his followers. The power of al-Qaeda weakened over the next years as new terrorist threats loomed on the horizon. In particular the Islamic State, or ISIS, who, like bin Laden before them, use the media to recruit new members and get their message to the world, has become more powerful. But the powerful Osama bin Laden and the organization he founded have been stopped. After nearly thirty years, bin Laden met the justice he so very much deserved at the hands of Americans, whom he so very much loathed.

## North Korea—the Hermit State

The communist nation of North Korea has always been a silent threat. Its threat comes from the fact that few are ever allowed into or out of the country, which has isolated itself from the

Supreme leader Kim Jong-un has continued his father's tight reign over North Korea.

world. Therefore, very little intelligence can be gathered about its military, its government, or what it is capable of.

Ever since the Korean War ended in armistice in 1953, North Korea shut its borders with its neighbor to the south, as well as against the rest of the world. As a communist regime took control of the country, it became shrouded in mystery. Kim Il-sung became the "supreme leader" of the Democratic People's Republic of Korea (DPRK), and his leadership was never questioned by the twenty-four million people who live in the cities and provinces of North Korea. Closed off from the rest of the world, there was very little intelligence about what was going on behind the closed communist doors. How were the people living? Were they thriving? Did they have enough to eat? How was their economy progressing? These questions and many more still remain unanswered.

What we do know is that the communist regime is enforced by state-issued propaganda that keeps its people in check. There are rumors about public executions, as well as starving people and abuse of power. But none of these can be proved true.

After the Cold War ended in the 1990s, the supreme leader of North Korea, Kim Il-sung, died. Videos of the people of North Korea crying in public, mourning the death of their leader were released to the Western media. But there was more to mourn than the death of their leader.

Without the backing of the communist Soviet Union, North Korea's economy plummeted. Food was scarce. And rumors abounded that North Korean citizens who disagreed with the totalitarian regime were imprisoned, tortured, and killed publicly. But the "hermit kingdom," as it is often called in the West, became more and more isolated, refusing to answer any questions posed by the UN or any other international agency.

Defectors from North Korea have shed a little light on the situation in North Korea. While the North Korean government uses propaganda to keep its citizens complacent, it is also true that we in the West hear a lot of negative propaganda against the communist nation. Many of this has been fueled by the stories of defectors—stories of rape, torture, false imprisonment, concentration camps, public executions, starving children, forced abortions, and basic human freedoms being torn away from the citizens of North Korea.

But as horrifying as these claims are, these are far less frightening than the North Korean army. Military personnel are revered in North Korea and considered the most important class of its citizenry. An estimated 16 percent of the population is in the military. The leaders of North Korea believe that a strong army is of the utmost importance in the state. To them, a strong nation cannot be powerful or independent without a strong military. And their military is armed to the teeth, including nuclear weapons.

North Korea has always been under nuclear threat. But the North Koreans see the United States as their biggest threat. North Korean children are taught revisionist history in school: that the United States had started the Korean War. They are taught that the West will one day attack. To them, it's not an issue of *if*. It's an issue of *when*. And it won't be China, or Japan, or Russia. It will be the United States. They are prepared to go to war with the United States and consider their army and their nuclear weapons self-defense against an imminent attack. They are taught that the United States is the cause of anything bad that happens in their lives. If their economy is bad, it is the fault of the United States. If they don't have enough food, it is because the United States has blocked food from entering their country. If a soldier dies, it is because he or she was serving the supreme leader in the conflict against the United States.

Few journalists or tourists have been allowed inside the last stronghold of communism. And those that are allowed are always accompanied by Korean government officials and given a very specific predetermined itinerary. This makes the truth a very difficult thing to acquire. What is known is that no US films, media, or television shows are allowed to be viewed in North Korea. All of their media is produced within the state, including all films, books, and newspapers. These are filled with propaganda that preaches against the United States and in favor of North Korean government and leaders. As a communist nation, everything is taken care of for the people by the government. The idea of communism is that are no people who are too rich or too poor. That everyone shares in the wealth of the state equally. Therefore, housing, education, medical care, food, and anything else that is needed for survival is provided for the individual. However, because of this the individual has no choice. They have no say in where they live, what kind of education they get, or what doctor they see. Their education is certainly filled with anti-Western sentiment, as well as propaganda supporting the greatness of their nation. Capitalism, which is the basis of most Western economies, is considered a poison for society.

Currently, the leader of North Korea is Kim Jong-un, the third in a dynasty of North Korean leaders. The people of this state consider themselves a large family and their leader is the father of their nation. Kim Jong-un makes a point of bragging to the world media about North Korea's nuclear power. In 2016, he said that North Korea had rockets that could easily reach the West Coast of the United States. Many videos have been released of Kim Jong-un watching as missiles are launched, and news programs in North Korea proclaimed them a success. The United Nations has condemned these actions, considering them a potential hostile act. But because of the iron curtain surrounding the hermit state, there is no proof about whether or not this is true. Surveillance has proved that North Korea does, in fact, have nuclear weapons as they claim. But whether or not they can launch them is another question, altogether.

In 2014, James Franco and Seth Rogen produced and starred in *The Interview*, a satirical comedy from Sony Pictures about two journalists going in to North Korea in an attempt to assassinate Kim Jong-un (played by Randall Park). The movie "touched a nerve" with North Korean officials who are notoriously paranoid about the safety of their leaders and nation. The Korean Central News Agency, the only media agency in North Korea, threatened severe and merciless action by the military of North Korea should the film be released. Because the film depicted the assassination of their supreme leader, as well as the fall of North Korea, it was considered an act of terrorism and war. They asked that the film be pulled. The original release date of the film was October 10. But the release of the film was pushed back to December 25.

On November 24, a group calling themselves "Guardians of Peace" hacked into the Sony Pictures database, releasing emails, employee information, and several unreleased films. A week before the film's release the group threatened to attack the film's New York City premiere. They asked that Sony pull the film, as well as it presence on the internet. Dan Sterling, writer of *The Interview*, said: "I couldn't believe that the most infamous man in the world knew about my script—but most importantly, I would never want something I wrote to lead to some kind of humanitarian disaster. I would be horrified if anyone got hurt over this." Seth Rogen, on the other hand, said the reason for the threats is that North Korean officials were afraid the film would actually make its way into North Korea. "They do have bootlegs and stuff. Maybe the tapes will make their way to North Korea and cause a revolution." Following the hack into Sony pictures and the threats to the safety of audiences, Franco and Rogen decided to pull the film, and Sony Pictures stopped all advertisement for the film. Changes were made to the film, including shortening Kim Jong-un's death scene, as well as design changes to costumes and characters. But the film was released online, including on Netflix, and became one of the most successful online distributions of the year.

Is it possible that North Korean officials felt so threatened by a satirical film that they hacked into a major corporation's database? Is it possible that they could make their threats against the United States come true? Is it possible that nuclear war with the Democratic People's Republic of Korea is on the horizon? The debate is active among journalists, political leaders, and experts. Some say that these are all hollow threats and that North Korea is merely bluffing about their power. Others claim that Kim Jong-un, an untested young leader with bravado, is unpredictable and very capable of starting a war with the United States. Still others say that North Korea will only further isolate itself from the rest of the world.

One thing is certain: there is a shroud of mystery around North Korea, its government, its policies, its military capabilities, and how its people live. The hermit kingdom may re-

## Abu Ghraib Prison Torture Scandal

Abu Ghraib prison is located in Iraq. It has held many prisoners captured during the war on terror since 2003. But it was soon determined by the US Army and the CIA that the treatment of prisoners there was not only inhumane, but was a violation of human rights. Amnesty International, a nongovernmental organization dedicated to the protection of human rights, concluded in 2003 that inmates in Abu Ghraib had been the victims of not only physical abuse (such as waterboarding, sleep deprivation, or beatings—all of which are illegal), but also sexual abuse, rape, torture, and in some cases, murder. Amnesty International and the Red Cross investigated further and determined that this was not a solitary case of some prison guards being drunk with power. They determined that this was a widespread pattern of abuse in many US-run prisons overseas. There were even allegations that these brutal actions were sanctioned by Secretary of State Donald Rumsfeld. The US government acknowledged the abuse, and there were even articles about it written for the Associated Press, with quotes from released prisoners about the abuse they had seen and experienced while imprisoned. But none of these reports seemed to garner much attention.

But in 2004, *60 Minutes II* did a piece on the abuse at Abu Ghraib. And now, physical evidence of the abuse was brought into American households. The segment showed photos of the inhumane treatment received by prisoners. Photos of prisoners being led around by leashes as they crawled naked on the floor. Photos of

Americans were shocked and disgusted when photographic evidence documenting the abuse of Abu Ghraib prisoners surfaced.

prisoners being covered with human feces, or being forced to hold urine soaked women's underwear on their faces, or being forced to masturbate publicly. One prisoner even died from a strapped hanging, a form of torture in which prisoners are hung by their wrists with their hands tied behind their back. Witnesses claimed they saw teenage boys being raped by their army guards or foreign objects being inserted into female prisoners. Some female prisoners even became pregnant from their rapes and were later killed by their family members in a tradition known as "honor killing." In some of the graphic photos that were released prisoners were made to create a pyramid with their naked bodies, while their prison guards—armed service men and women—stood behind them, smiling.

The world was stunned to find that their service men and women could be involved in something so disgusting and degrading to human beings. After all, wasn't that one of the reasons the nation had gone to war—to stop acts like this from being committed?

The media and much of the public were outraged and demanded Rumsfeld's resignation. They were upset that the Bush Administration had allowed this to happen and had denied that it was happening for so long.

Legal action was swift. The US Department of Defense removed seventeen soldiers from their posts at Abu Ghraib. Eleven of these soldiers were convicted of committing crimes against humanity and dereliction of duty. Most only received light sentences, but their military careers were finished. In 2006, Congress passed the Military Commissions Act, which essentially made it impossible for detainees to challenge any of the crimes committed against them while they are in custody.

But the media, Amnesty International, the United Nations, and many other international organizations have kept a close watch over Abu Ghraib and other US prisons abroad. It was later revealed that many settlements had been doled out to prisoners as a way to buy their silence. It has also been determined that while torture is a common practice of obtaining information from prisoners, there must be perimeters set for this torture. As of today, reports of torture and abuse continue to come out from international prisons around the world. But nothing quite as shocking and degrading as what occurred at Abu Ghraib. In order to prevent something like that from ever happening again, the military needs to be diligent in keeping an eye on their personnel and making sure such an abuse of power is never allowed to occur.

main a mystery for years to come. But it must also be noted: a mysterious nation that makes threats against another country is nothing to be trifled with. Because, in fact, it may be more than bravado. They very well could have the capabilities to start a war. And they certainly think it would be justified.

## D-Day Deception

Perhaps the biggest military secret of all time, the Normandy landings, codenamed Operation Neptune, better known as D-Day, was more than just a military invasion. It was the work of a complicated network of double and triple agencies working for Great Britain, feeding false information to Nazi officials in order to gain a foothold in occupied France.

The plan, at its core was rather simple: to invade France and push the Nazi army back to Berlin. But with hundreds of thousands of troops occupying France, Poland, and much of Europe, the Allied forces had much to contend with. But Winston Churchill had a plan: deception.

Tar Robertson was a Scottish born MI5 intelligence officer who was in control of a network of spies. This network of spies was all double or triple agents—many sent from the Germans themselves in order to gain intelligence about the British military agenda. In fact, as it turned out, every single spy sent by Germany was actually under control of British intelligence. And they would prove invaluable in the defeat of the Germans.

Five agents in particular were especially helpful in this campaign. These five agents were absolutely trusted by Hitler and other German officials, and their information was taken as absolutely true. These five agents had managed to convince the Germans that they were loyal Nazis, eager to help the Third Reich.

In November of 1944, Winston Churchill, along with many other Allied leaders, had a conclave to determine the best way to gain back control of Europe. Their plan? To convince Hitler and the Germans that Allied forces would invade the heavily fortified Callais, in the north of France, and distract the German army from their real target: Normandy, a beach much farther south and much less protected. As the plan was hatched, it was soon realized that this secret was of utmost importance to the Allies winning the war. The plan was given the name Operation Bodyguard and its main mission was to protect the plan to invade Normandy.

Five double agents were integral to this plan.

Nathalie Sergueiew (Lily Sergeyev), code name Treasure, was a beautiful Russian-born French woman who used her wiles and charm to make her way into German intelligence. She was sent to England to spy on British intelligence. Once there, she immediately turned against the Germans and began working for the British. Her job was to go around the countryside and collect information. Then, she would send this "chicken feed," or snippets of truth, half-truths, and lies back to her German handler.

Joan Pujol García, codename Garbo, was a Spanish-born inventor with a wild imagination. He managed to convince his German handler that he not only was a committed Nazi with access to British intelligence, but also that he had an intricate network of twenty-seven spies at his disposal, including an army officer, a secretary, and a group of Welsh fascists. However, all twenty-seven of these individuals were made up by Garbo, who worked tirelessly to convince the Germans of the intelligence he had gathered through his fake network.

Roman Czerniawski, codename Brutus, was an officer in the Polish military and was a triple agent. He was originally a spy for the British on the Germans. But once he was captured, he pretended to turn his coat and spy on the British. In actuality he was spying once more on the Germans.

Elvira Chaudoir, codename Bronx, was a Peruvian bisexual party girl whose job, according to the Germans, was to haunt fancy cocktail parties and casinos in order to gather gossip and information from high-ranking officials. She sent letters to her handler in Germany using invisible ink to write messages between the lines of correspondence.

Dusko Popov, codename Tricycle, had the most dangerous job of all: he had direct contact with German officials, and had to, therefore, be the most charming and convincing of all. He worked closely with his best friend Johnny Jebsen, codename Artist, who was also a double agent for the Germans. In fact, it was Jebsen who discovered that all the German spies in England were actually working for England.

The job of these men and women? To convince their German spymasters that the Allied forces were planning an attack on Callais, or even Norway to the north.

The plan began with simple tidbits of information sent along to the Germans. Treasure informed her handler that a large American army was assembling in Kent, pointed directly across the channel from Callais. To support this, inflatable tanks and dummy aircraft were assembled in the English countryside and placed there, so that any German reconnaissance planes might see what appeared to be a large show of force. General Patton, whom Hitler widely regarded as his more formidable enemy, was also sent to Kent.

Garbo sent over five hundred messages to his German handlers, informing them of the threat to Callais and urging them to send German reinforcements to the region. His handlers listened.

Brutus informed his spymasters about a threat to Norway. In order to back this claim, Allied forces set up another dummy army on the Northeast coast of Scotland. In response, Germans sent more forces to the coast of Norway— and away from the beaches at Normandy.

Bronx also sent messages to her handlers about a possible invasion at the Bay of Biscay, in southern France. In response, German troops were sent there, as well.

Tricycle had the most perilous job of all—convincing his German handlers, face-to-face, that his information was true.

But, as the day of the invasion came closer and closer, some of the threads in the intricate knot of lies began to unravel.

Agent Artist was summoned by his German superiors, and told he was going to receive accommodation for his good work. Instead, he was beaten, kidnapped, and smuggled out of Lisbon, Portugal, back to Berlin, where he was tortured. When Tricycle told Tar Robinson of this news, there was an immediate fear that since Agent Artist knewsabout the imminent invasion of Normandy and the

Allied forces landed at Omaha Beach in Normandy, France, during World War II. The secret military operation surprised Germany.

fact that all of the German spies in Britain were actually working for the crown, their elaborate plan would be revealed.

Agent Treasure, whose greatest love in the world was her dog, Babs, also delivered a devastating blow to the plan. Babs had been held under quarantine in Gibraltar, and just when she was about to get her beloved terrier back, news broke that the dog had been run over. Treasure immediately told her handler that she had been given a secret code by the Germans to inform them if she had been compromised. She didn't tell her English handlers whether or not she had used it. But she did tell them that it would be her revenge for the death of her dog.

In order to counteract anything that the Germans may have gleaned from agents Treasure or Artist, the other spies flooded the Nazis with information about an imminent attack on Callais. But all of this information depended on the Fuehrer's belief. Even though Hitler had many great tacticians and military men in his employ the ultimate decision about what to do with the troops was his. And by some miracle, Hitler believed that the threat to Callais was real. He bolstered troops in the area.

But on June 6, 1944, the largest amphibious attack in history began. One hundred and fifty thousand troops broke onto the shores of Normandy Beach and devastated the German forces there, who were unprepared for an attack. Ten thousand Allied soldiers died that day, but the number would have been far greater had the Germans known what to expect. Allied forces finally had a foothold in France, and they began pushing north.

Still, the spies' work was not done. They told their handlers that the invasion of Normandy was a diversionary tactic and that Callais was still under threat of invasion. Even a month later, it was proved that the Germans believed this information to be true. Agent Garbo was even given an Iron Cross by the Nazis for his work as a spy.

It was only decades after the war was over that the spies

revealed their work for the Allies. Most retired to quiet lives in Allied countries, surrounded by their children and animals. Garbo even went on to become a sheep farmer. But their efforts were a turning point in the war and saved thousands of lives in the process. These brave men and women and their jobs as double and triple agents brought down the Nazi regime and stopped it from destroying humanity.

## The Manhattan Project

Over sixty years have elapsed since the vision of a mushroom cloud of smoke rising over a Japanese city called Hiroshima burned itself forever on the human consciousness. In that split second, man unleashed the forces of nature that he had learned to harness in the United States' most top-secret research, and, as a result, the nuclear age was born. After that explosion, nothing would ever be the same again. The world now lay split into two camps, each with enough nuclear hardware to make the Hiroshima bomb look like a firecracker.

The United States developed the bomb under conditions of amazing secrecy in a research program called the Manhattan Project. Led by brilliant physicist Dr. Robert Oppenheimer, the Americans were engaged in a frantic race against time—for in a world at war, Nazi Germany was also engaged in its own research to split the atom. Although behind the US effort, the fact that Hitler's scientists were engaged in research made President Franklin Roosevelt aware that, no matter what the cost, the free world had to achieve the first atom bomb and thereby completely ensure its supremacy over the forces of Germany and Japan.

It was the rise of Nazism and the war which caused groups of European scientists, many of them Jewish, to flee to the United States. As early as 1933, these brilliant men and women warned that Nazi scientists had been given huge budget increases to pursue the dream of a controlled nuclear reaction: in effect, a bomb of awesome power. In 1938, US intelligence learned that outside Berlin, in a closely guarded laboratory, German physicists had succeeded in splitting a single atom. They had not harnessed its energy, but they were well on the way. It was enough to spur the most eminent physicist of this, or any age, to write to the president of the United States urging him to quickly push for nuclear research.

Albert Einstein, father of the theory of relativity, was one of those banished from Nazi Germany because he was a Jew. He wrote an impassioned letter to Roosevelt, who was still struggling to rebuild the US economy from the days of the Great Depression, which had devastated the United States. The plea from such an eminent scientist shocked Roosevelt and moved him to order research effort on the bomb. Even though the United States was neutral in the war until 1941, Roosevelt and his advisers were of the opinion that the prize of nuclear supremacy should belong to the mightiest industrial nation.

Since the turn of the century, scientists had known that the element uranium naturally disintegrated by emitting alpha particles containing neutrons and protons; a process yielding a spectacular million times more energy per atom than ordinary fire. The only problem was that the process took millions of years as part of the natural evolutionary process of earth. What if that process could be sped up, harnessed, and unleashed? The prospect for scientists was breathtaking and frightening.

Enrico Fermi, an Italian scientist who came to the United States in 1938 from Mussolini's Italy, was awarded the 1938 Nobel Prize for his research into atomic energy and shortly afterward came to America to take up a teaching post at Columbia University. Fermi learned there of the German experiment in Berlin. Together with several eminent scientists from around

The atomic bomb dropped on Hiroshima, Japan, decimating the city and effectively ending the war.

the world, he began his first experiments into nuclear fission.

Fermi was one of the first scientists to throw a veil of secrecy around the research. In the early days it was an academic project, not sanctioned by the government or military. He had to warn his colleagues, who were long used to trading information with other scientists and boasting of their progress in scientific journals, to remain silent. The military later complained that the security in those early days was "leaking like a sieve."

Before building a bomb, the scientists first had to learn how to split the atom and harness its energy. By mid-1938, President Roosevelt had authorized the Manhattan Project as a government funded program and realizing the need for secrecy, decreed that the separate research programs were to be carried out at sites and locations spaced widely apart. A secret bunker complex was carved out of the desert in New Mexico, where it was ultimately hoped the bomb would be tested. The research into splitting the atom was carried out under Fermi's guidance in Chicago.

The breakthrough came on December 3, 1942, on a sports field in Chicago. Fermi assembled his research team with the device that would trigger a nuclear chain reaction, the first step to forming the "critical mass" that becomes the nuclear explosion. The scientists had built a nuclear "pile," a primitive nuclear reactor designed to test whether nuclear energy could be triggered in a chain reaction and harnessed for energy. The reactor took the form of a spheroid shape, packed with uranium, which would be bombarded with neutrons and protons as safety rods inserted into the device were removed one by one. On hand was a "suicide squad" of firefighters armed with nothing more than a few buckets of water to put out Earth's first manmade nuclear fire if the chain reaction were so violent that it caught fire!

The sports field had been sealed off for 3 miles (4.8 kilometers) around by police and security agents desperate to shield the experiment that was taking place. Anyone wishing to go near the place was told that soil samples for a new government farming program were being taken.

One by one the rods were pulled. Fermi witnessed the Geiger counters monitoring the berserk levels of radiation as they pulsed through the sphere, triggering the massive chain reaction. "Throw in the safety rods!" cried Fermi at the last minute before the sphere looked likely to explode in that most dangerous of nuclear accidents—meltdown. The experiment worked and Fermi celebrated man's arrival in the atomic age with a bottle of Chianti.

However, just as the Manhattan Project got underway properly in 1942, building the bomb in the desert complex, some of the physicists engaged became worried about the nature of their tasks. They were concerned with the nuclear destruction that they might be unleashing on the world. It was a question of conscience that caused more than one scientist to leave the project and gave a security headache to the agencies concerned with keeping secret the most important research of the war. All the scientists involved were required to sign secrecy oaths. But for good measure, many were kept under the scrutiny of the military for months afterward.

The military man in charge of the project was a bluff brigadier general named Leslie Groves. He was used to giving orders and used to having them obeyed. He, more than anyone, impressed on the men of science the need to keep the project a secret. He pointed out that one of the prizes that fell to the German war machine in 1940 during the battle of Norway was the Norsky Hydro Hydrogen Electrolysis plant, which manufactured heavy water, which is the most efficient substance, say scientists, for the construction of a chain-reacting atomic pile. Although the plant was later crippled in an Allied commando raid, Groves told the scientists, "Make it quicker, without being caught, and we'll have them. Don't and they will have us." The work progressed with everyone involved aware of the need for urgency.

The giant DuPont company was given the government order to manufacture enough plutonium for the bomb. Government contracts everywhere for the manufacture of the weapon were disguised as something else—research into pesticides, research into solar power, and research into alternative fuels. The steel delivered for some of the prototype bomb casings was marked down as steel for artillery barrels.

By 1945, a prototype had been developed and, by July, was ready for testing. In the middle of the New Mexico desert, Operation Trinity, the code name for the testing, was set for July 16. The bomb was called Fat Man and the site for its testing was 10 miles (16 km) from the Alamogordo Air Base, a complex of underground bunkers and buildings where much of the construction of the bomb had been carried out.

A host of military and scientific top brass were assembled to witness the largest explosion ever made by man on Earth. At 5:30 a.m. in the cold drizzle, a ball of fire reaching 41,000 feet (12, 496 km) (12,000 feet [3, 657 km]higher than the tallest mountain) soared above the desert. The thunder from the explosion reverberated across the open spaces, shaking the ground as if an earthquake were about to consume the earth. Oppenheimer, in that fearful moment, recited two verses from Sanskrit, the ancient language of India. One was: "If the radiance of a thousand suns were to burst into the sky, that would be the splendor of the mighty one." The second was: "I am become Death, the shatterer of worlds."

Three months before the test, the most secret airfield ever constructed was built at Tinian, a Pacific island situated near Japan. The inhabitants of the island were completely isolated from the world as teams of engineers and construction workers carved out the forward atomic base from where an elite air wing, the 509th, would be based to carry out the nuclear attack on Japan. President Harry Truman had sanctioned an American nuclear assault on the Japanese mainland in an effort to save American lives as Japanese troops fought fanatically to the death in their bid to hold their ground. The 509th was formed in conditions of such secrecy that even the top ranking scientists and officers on the Manhattan Project did not know that a squadron with the sole purpose of delivering the bomb to Japan had been formed.

The secrecy surrounding the bomb and the delivery of atomic material to Tinian for final bomb assembly had tragic consequences. The cruiser *Indianapolis* loaded with the radioactive cargo sailed from San Francisco to Tinian and on its return voyage was torpedoed. Because its mission was so secret the naval command did not know its exact position or whereabouts. As a result nearly four hundred men died in the shark-infested waters before any rescue vessels were sent to their aid. It was one of the war's prime examples where secrecy overrode every consideration— including human life.

The plane that was to carry the bomb was to be piloted by the United States' top flyer, Captain Paul Tibbets, who named the B-29 bomber the *Enola Gay* after his mother. On August 6, 1954, Mrs. Tibbets achieved fame of a kind when the bomb was dropped on Hiroshima. In the blinding light of the nuclear explosion, equivalent of 20,000 tons of TNT, 150,000 people were incinerated, thousands more suffering the appalling burns of radiation.

The Manhattan Project was successful, but Robert Oppenheimer was right— he had become the shatterer of worlds.

# CHAPTER FIVE: SECRETS OF THE STARS

## NATALIE WOOD

Natalie Wood was one of the best-known actresses of her day. She stared in such classics as *Rebel without a Cause*, *Miracle on 34th Street*, *Splendor in the Grass*, and perhaps most famously, as Maria in *West Side Story*. She received three Academy Awards (Oscars) before she had even turned twenty-five.

In 1956, when she was eighteen years old, Wood met the twenty-six-year-old actor Robert Wagner, a Hollywood heart-throb. The studio had arranged their date for publicity. But Wood fell hard for Wagner, and Wagner fell for her in turn. They were married a year later, in 1957. The marriage wouldn't last however, and they divorced in April 1962.

Wood then dated British producer Richard Gregson, even though he was married at the time. Once his divorce was finalized, the two married in 1969. They had one daughter in 1970, Natasha. Wood made the choice then to focus on her family more than her career. But shortly after her daughter was born, she overheard an explicit phone call between her husband and her secretary. Wood and Gregson divorced in April 1972, which began a time of separation between Wood and her family, who thought she should stay with her husband for the sake of their newborn daughter.

Wood ignored this advice and began seeing Wagner again. They married five months later, in July of 1972. They had another daughter two years later. Theirs was a Hollywood romance that seemed to be actually working. The couple was devoted to each other and their children, and even though they were a power couple, it seemed as though they were genuinely in love.

Robert Wagner and Natalie Wood's relationship ended with her death. Mysteries surrounding her drowning remain today.

But seven years later, tragedy struck. While filming *Brainstorm* in 1981, she went on a boating trip with Wagner and costar Christopher Walken. Although Wagner was an experienced boater, they hired a captain, Dennis Davern, to man the vessel. It was smooth sailing on that warm autumn day of November 28. There were rumors that the marriage between Wood and Wagner was no longer as happy as it once had been. There were also rumors she was having an affair with Walken. As they sailed around Santa Catalina Island in California, it seemed like any other day for the Hollywood stars. But then, according to her husband, Natalie Wood disappeared.

According to Wagner, his wife had gone into the stateroom of the yacht, while he went to the cabin. When he went to join her in the stateroom, he discovered she wasn't there, and that the ship's dinghy was also gone. When Wood didn't return within a few minutes, he took a small cruising boat to look for her. Having no success, he called the Coast Guard.

Wood's body was discovered the next day, dressed in her nightgown and floating face down in a lagoon near some cliffs on Santa Catalina Island. An inflatable raft was found not far from her body. Wagner immediately returned to their home in Beverly

Hills after identifying his wife's body. Natalie Wood was buried in the Westwood Village Memorial Park Cemetery very soon after the autopsy was finished.

It all seems very plausible, except for a few key factors. Wood was quoted to have said just a few weeks before her demise: "I'm frightened to death of the water…I can swim a little bit, but I'm afraid of water that is dark." And what husband wouldn't immediately call for help upon discovering that his wife had gone missing? Wagner later admitted that after a night of drinking he, Walken, and Wood had been arguing before his wife disappeared. Surely that also seemed suspicious.

The coroner concluded that Wood's death was accidental. He stated that she must have untied the dinghy, slipped, hit her head, and drowned. But why would a woman who was terrified of dark water voluntarily go out in it? Some posited that perhaps it had been beating up against the side of the *Splendor*, and Wood had gone out to secure it when she slipped. The autopsy also revealed that Wood's blood alcohol level was 0.14 percent, and there were traces of two medications in her bloodstream: a motion-sickness pill and a painkiller, both of which increase the effects of alcohol. But the cause of death was undoubtedly drowning and hypothermia.

Fans, experts, and inquiring minds continued to probe the investigation into Natalie Wood's death. In 2011, the case was reopened. At this time the coroner changed the cause of death to "drowning and other undetermined factors." The recent report also states that they were unable to determine how Wood ended up in the water. But nothing else has been said about the case. It was determined that there was no investigation of the yacht itself, of if there had been, there is no longer a record of it. Investigators should have checked for signs of a struggle, or, at the very least, some sort of evidence of Wood's having hit her head.

In 2014, another addendum was added to the autopsy report stating that some of the bruises found on her body might have happened before she went into the water, but they couldn't prove this conclusively. They also finally investigated the yacht, albeit thirty-five years later. The investigation turned up no new evidence, although the case may never truly be closed.

Many theorize that Robert Wagner killed his wife. Wagner continues to maintain his innocence, even discussing the matter in depth in his 2008 memoir *Pieces of My Heart*. Is it possible that a beloved Hollywood star killed his wife, who was a star in her own right? Is it possible that the LAPD helped to cover up this murder? Thirty-five years later, the investigation has been reopened, and there are many who think the answers are out there, if investigators look in the right places. Until then, the death of Natalie Wood remains one of Hollywood's biggest unsolved mysteries.

## The Curse of Twenty-Seven

Also known as the "27 Club", there seems to be something that happens to many young celebrities at the age of twenty-seven— they die. The curse of twenty-seen seems to particularly befall musicians at the peak of their fame. These artists' stars rise even farther after their deaths, and many of them will live on in infamy not just for the music they created, but because their lives were cut tragically short.

### Jimi Hendrix (November 27, 1942 – September 18, 1970)

Widely regarded as the best guitarist of his generation, Jimi Hendrix shot to fame in London in 1966 with his band The Jimi Hendrix Experience. Known for his bluesy influence and psychedelic sound, Hendrix became one of the brightest stars at the Woodstock Music Festival in New York in 1969, when he played the "Star-Spangled Banner" in a new, rock n' roll way.

Like many musicians of the time, Hendrix experimented with drugs and alcohol. In the early days of his career, it was mostly beer and marijuana. But as the pressures of stardom increased, along with the racism he faced in the United States and the UK, his substance use turned into abuse. Usually soft-spoken and mild-mannered, Hendrix was known for getting violent when he combined heavy drugs with alcohol. He was arrested in Sweden in 1968 for getting into a fight in a hotel bar. He was arrested again in 1969 for carrying heroin and hashish into Canada.

On the morning of September 18, 1970, Monika Dannemann, Hendrix's girlfriend, awoke to find him breathing, but unconscious, beside her. She called an ambulance, which arrived a few minutes later. He was taken to St Mary Abbot's Hospital, where he was declared dead at 12:48 p.m. Dannemann claimed they'd spent the day together on September 17 and had done nothing more than have dinner and share a bottle of wine. But an autopsy revealed that Hendrix had breathed in his own vomit and died of asphyxia while intoxicated with barbiturates. Hendrix was buried near his mother in Greenwood Cemetery in Renton, Washington, close to his hometown of Seattle.

Hendrix's influence on music is beyond doubt. He received several posthumous Grammy awards, as well as an induction into the Rock and Roll Hall of Fame, and a star on the Hollywood Walk of Fame. But perhaps his most living legacy is the influence he had on other artists. Prince, George Clinton, the Red Hot Chili Peppers, the Beastie Boys, Run DMC, Stevie Ray Vaughn, and many more all note Hendrix as one of their biggest influences. But to Hendrix, a legend in his own time, it was music that was the most important. He believed in the power of music,and that it could change minds, hearts, and souls: "Music doesn't lie. If there is something to be changed in this world, then it can only happen through music."

## Janis Joplin (January 19, 1943 – October 4, 1970)

Perhaps one of the most influential female vocalists in the history of rock n' roll, Janis Joplin's famous raspy, heartrending voice is one that will haunt many musicians and fans for years to come. She shot to fame on the San Francisco music scene with her band Big Brother and the Holding Company, with the aid of film producers at the Monterey Pop Festival in 1967 when was just twenty-four years old.

Joplin had always been a troubled young woman: insecure and bullied, she didn't feel beautiful. But she was determined to be different and put forth a tough exterior. As she became more and more famous for her unique voice and style she, like many others at the time, began experimenting with drugs—specifically heroin. She struggled with addiction for years, but in 1970, life was going well for Janis. She had a successful solo career, and she was recording a new album, entitled *Pearl*. She was in love and ready to face the next chapter. She was getting clean.

But on October 4, she shot up with heroin for the last time. Perhaps as a last hurrah, or perhaps to calm her mind that was once again spiraling into depression. It is unclear whether it was her dosage or the fact that it was coupled with alcohol, but Joplin was discovered dead by producer Paul Rothchild at the Landmark Motor Hotel in Hollywood, where Joplin had been staying. Once again, the music community mourned another life cut far too short. Her album was released posthumously and sold better than any of her previous works. Songs such as "Me and Bobby McGee," "Cry Baby," and "A Woman Left Lonely" rocketed to the top of the charts. In 1995, Joplin was inducted into the Rock and Roll Hall of Fame, proving that her music was still very much in the American consciousness. In 2014, she was given a star on the Hollywood Walk of

Fame. She was even given a commemorative stamp by the US Postal Service. But none of these will make up for the tragic loss of a talent that shone too brightly, a jewel of a woman known as "Pearl."

## Jim Morrison (December 8, 1943 – July 3, 1971)

Widely regarded as one of the most influential frontmen in rock n' roll history, Jim Morrison was a songwriter, poet, and singer. His extravagant performances and lifestyle made him an icon in his lifetime, while his death catapulted him into infamy.

After graduating from UCLA, Morrison began living a bohemian lifestyle in Venice Beach, California, living off canned beans, LSD, and alcohol. At this time, he met the other members of the band that would soon become The Doors. As the band jammed together and wrote songs, Morrison delved deeper into substance use. In 1967, the band signed with Elektra records and began to make it in the public eye. The svelte singer was known for electrifying performances and wearing leather pants. In March of 1969, he attempted to start a riot at a Miami concert. He failed, but he was charged with indecent exposure. He carried on many well-known love affairs and became known for his spoken-word poetry and his outlandish behavior.

On July 3, 1971, Jim Morrison was found dead in the bathtub of his apartment in Paris, France. He'd moved there a few months earlier and was going on long walks and apparently trying to get himself together. There was no autopsy performed by French officials, but his cause of death was ruled as "heart failure." It is assumed, however, that heroin was involved: possibly that he had inhaled it, thinking it was cocaine. His girlfriend at the time of his death, Pamela Courson, gave many contradictory stories about Morrison's death, leaving many to assume she had something to do with his death. Courson died of an accidental heroin overdose three years later, leaving many questions in her wake. She was also twenty-seven when she died.

Morrison was buried in Père Lachaise Cemetery in Paris, a huge tourist attraction in the city, where many other celebrities and artists are buried. Many headstones and plaques have been placed on the grave over the years, including a bust created by Croatian sculptor Mladen Mikulin on the tenth anniversary of the singer's death. The bust was defaced many times over the years, before being removed in 1988. Afterward, the singer's father had a simple headstone created for his son, with a simple bronze plaque that reads: *KATA TON DAIMONA EAYTOY*. In Greek: "according to his own daemon." Or put simply: "he lived true to himself."

## Jean-Michel Basquiat (December 22, 1960 – August 12, 1988)

Jean-Michael Basquiat is perhaps the man who can be credited with making street art mainstream. He brought it into the public eye outside of urban cities. He started his career in the 1970s on the Lower East Side of Manhattan. Common themes in his work were wealth versus poverty, integration versus segregation, and inner versus outer experience. He also worked with mixed media, incorporating poetry, words, images, and historical and modern imagery. He became well known in New York City and caught the attention of international art critics and other artists.

But, like many artists, Basquiat had a dark side. He'd grown up poor, and had a rough childhood. And the downtown art scene in the late 1970s and early 1980s offered escape in the form of drugs. After his collaborator and mentor Andy Warhol died in 1987, Basquiat became more and more isolated and spiraled into severe drug use. He attempted to overcome his substance abuse, but on August 12, 1988, he was discovered in his studio on Great Jones Street in Manhattan, dead from an overdose of cocaine and heroin, known as "speedballing."

The art world was sent reeling. Basquiat was buried in Brooklyn's Greenwood Cemetery. Hundreds of artists came to his memorial service in November, including hip-hop pioneer Fab 5 Freddy, the musicians John Lurie and Arto Lindsay, artist Keith Haring, and poet David Shapiro. Many modern artists, musicians, and writers have recognized Basquiat's influence, including Jay Z, Kanye West, Macklemore, Fall Out Boy, and many more. His art has inspired fashion lines, as well as generations of artists to continue creating in his unique urban style. His art is among the best selling in the world. An untitled piece of Basquiat's art sold at Christie's for $57.3 million to a Japanese collector in 2016. Many of his pieces can still be seen displayed in museums around the world, including the Whitney Museum of American Art.

## Kurt Cobain (February 20, 1967 – April 5, 1994)

It is hard to discuss American pop culture without mentioning the iconic voice of Generation X: Kurt Cobain. He was a masterful songwriter, singer, and musician and the inspiration for a pop culture revolution in the 1990s.

Born in Aberdeen, Washington, the first years of Cobain's life were idyllic—he was described as a happy, artistic child who loved music from an early age. But when his parents divorced when he was eight years old, his innocence was shattered. Both parents remarried, and Kurt no longer felt important to either of them. He suffered with bouts of depression early in life and began smoking marijuana as a young teen. High school was a difficult time for the budding musician. He

Nirvana frontman Kurt Cobain shocked the world when he became a member of the notorious 27 Club in 1994.

wasn't able to keep his grades up, and he eventually dropped out. Shortly after, his mother kicked him out, and he was left to wander the streets of Aberdeen.

In 1987, everything changed for Cobain: he met friend and bassist Krist Novoselic, who would help Cobain become the artist he wanted to become. By all accounts, Kurt seemed aimless in his personal life, but as Novoselic and Cobain began the band Nirvana, it was clear that Cobain was laser-focused on his music. He was serious about rehearsals and direction. He was a perfectionist and a demanding leader. After a period of shuffling through Seattle-area drummers, Nirvana signed with Sub Pop Records in 1988, and released their first album, *Bleach*. Although it was an indie record that had songs mostly played on college radio stations, it was a hit. Nirvana went on an international tour in 1989.

Although Cobain was serious about his music, it is clear he was never meant to be a rock star. He was always sickly, suffering from stomach problems, depression, and many other health issues. On the last leg of their tour in Rome, Cobain was upset at the way the band sounded. Always the perfectionist, he had a nervous breakdown on stage and threatened to jump from the 30 ft (9m) speakers on stage to kill himself. After returning from the tour, Cobain tried to rest, but a series of romances and breakups left him emotionally shattered. But from heartache often comes the best music.

In 1991, Nirvana finally found a drummer that could enhance their sound: Dave Grohl. After months of writing and recording, they released the album *Nevermind*,and their first major single "Smells Like Teen Spirit." The song rocketed to the top of the charts, even knocking Michael Jackson from the number one spot. Kurt Cobain became an idol for angsty teens everywhere. Fans began to dress like him and try to emulate him. Nirvana's once half-empty shows were now sold out at bigger venues. Being in the spotlight was hard on the frontman, who liked his private life to be just that. Cobain began experimenting with harder drugs, specifically heroin. It was his way of coping with the limelight that had suddenly been thrust upon him. It made him feel alive again. And it would, eventually, be the thing that killed him.

In 1992, he met and married the lead singer of punk band Hole, Courtney Love. Cobain had already overdosed on heroin once when they discovered she was pregnant. Love wanted Cobain to get clean before their baby was born. In early August 1992, Cobain checked himself into a rehabilitation center at Cedars-Sinai Hospital in Los Angeles, California. On August 18, his daughter, Francis Bean, was born in the same hospital. Many wondered if they, who were known for their rock-star lifestyles and drug abuse, were fit parents. An investigation was performed by social services, and the couple were deemed "unfit parents" when rumors surfaced that Francis Bean had been born with drug-related health issues. It took seven months, but the couple was finally granted full custody in 1993. Fatherhood and marriage seemed to make Cobain happy for the first time in his life. He was a doting father who enjoyed the domestic bliss that appeared to the world to be right out of a punk-rock fairy tale. Shortly after, Nirvana released their third album, *In Utero*, which sold over five million copies in its first weeks of sale. Following the success of the album, Nirvana was approached by MTV to do an acoustic set for their television series *Unplugged*. This is considered arguably the best performance of Cobain's career.

But despite commercial and familial success, Cobain was still struggling. His drug abuse escalated, with band members and producers saying that it was rare to see Cobain sober. In October, Nirvana began another grueling international tour. After months of traveling and playing shows, Cobain checked into a hotel in Rome. His wife and daughter had joined him. On March 2, 1994, Courtney Love awoke to discover Cobain unconscious and bleeding from his nose. A three-page suicide note was found near his body. She immediately called an ambulance. His stomach was pumped and it was determined that he had taken over fifty pills of Rohypnol with alcohol. He was in a coma for twenty hours before being revived. The rest of the tour was cancelled, and Cobain went home to Seattle with his family.

But his near-death experience did nothing to change Cobain's habits. He ignored an intervention held by his friends and family, continuing his severe drug abuse. In April 1994, he checked into a rehab facility in Los Angeles, but disappeared two days later. Despite all attempts to find him, Cobain had vanished. On April 8, 1994, Cobain was discovered in the greenhouse above the garage of his Seattle, Washington home, dead from an apparent self-inflicted gunshot wound. Near his body were his wallet and a suicide note.

Fans around the world mourned the loss of their idol and the voice of their generation. Nirvana's record sales shot through the roof. Many impromptu services and memorials were held in parks, churches, and basements around the world over the coming months. A final memorial service was held on May 31, 1999, in which daughter Francis Bean scattered her father's ashes into McLane Creek in Olympia, Washington, as a Buddhist monk chanted prayers.

He is consistently ranked as one of the greatest musicians and songwriters of all time. In 2005, the city of Aberdeen, Washington, erected a sign at its border. It reads "Welcome to Aberdeen, Washington. Come as you are."

But the case of Kurt Cobain's death simply will not die. Not only do many fans believe his death may have been a conspiracy, but some investigators do as well. Courtney Love hired private investigator Tom Grant just a few days before Cobain's death. She expressed concern about him since he was missing, had access to firearms and drugs, and was suicidal. She even filed a police report with the Seattle Police Department after he left the rehab facility in LA, claiming to be his mother, Wendy O'Connor. Many experts say that the investigation into Cobain's death was botched and that the police department had jumped to conclusions about the circumstances surrounding Cobain's death. He had a lethal dose of heroin in his system, toxicology reports stated, nearly five times the amount it would take for even the heaviest of users to die. It was determined that there was 1.52mg per liter of blood in Cobain's body, which means he would have had to have injected almost 230mg of heroin. Most users, even heavy addicts like Cobain, only inject about 30-40mg. If he had that level of heroin in his blood stream, some experts say, he would have been unconscious: unable to put away his heroin kit and pick up a shotgun, much less pull the trigger. Other investigators say that the angle in which the shotgun was found in Cobain's hands isn't plausible, considering where the shotgun shell was found at the crime scene. Others still posit that the police department was paid off to cover up the potential crime, as photographs from the scene weren't developed, and investigators waited thirty days to process the fingerprints on the shotgun.

Many have suggested that Courtney Love, jealous of her husband's success, as well as upset about the status of their marriage, had planned the murder of her husband. Rumors had surrounded the couple for months about a breakup, and Love was known to be a jealous woman. Many also posit that the rambling suicide note, found in a planter in the greenhouse with a red pen, may have been written by Courtney.

In March 2014, the photographs were finally developed and released to the media in the weeks preceding the twentieth anniversary of Cobain's death. The photos were heartbreaking to fans, who saw for the first time the exact images of their hero's death. Although the investigation has still been ruled a suicide, the case was never truly closed. The Seattle Police Department still receives inquiries and tips on a weekly basis about the death of Kurt Cobain, proving, once more, just what an influence he had on pop culture and his fans.

It's been over twenty years since his tragic death, but Kurt Cobain will remain forever in the consciousness of American music fans. His influence can still be heard in artists today, and many books, films, documentaries, and posthumous tributes have been dedicated to him, including a surprise performance between the surviving members of Nirvana with legendary musician Paul McCartney in 2013. We may never know the truth about Kurt Cobain's death—the only person who could tell us is the man himself. But it is clear that it was a life cut tragically short at the height of his fame, probably because the spotlight was just a little too bright for such a sensitive soul. His last words to the public, written in his suicide note stated: "It is better to burn out than to fade away."

## Amy Winehouse (September 14, 1983 – July 23, 2011)

English songstress Amy Winehouse was best known for her expressive voice, her unique style, and her ability to mix genres to create something totally new. Widely considered to be a musical prodigy, Winehouse began her early career writing songs and performing with orchestras, at jazz clubs, and at bars in England. She was offered a record contract in 2000, when she was just seventeen years old. As she was being groomed to become a star, her producers and agents kept her an industry secret, waiting for the right moment to reveal her truly spectacular talent.

In 2003, her debut album, *Frank*, was released to rave reviews. It went on to receive platinum sales after performances at the Glastonbury Festival and the Montreal International Jazz Festival. But the pressures of maintaining her stardom were hard for Amy to handle. She turned to alcohol and drugs to release the pressure and the depression she felt after her grandmother died in 2006. Winehouse was often seen intoxicated in public and was losing weight rapidly and dramatically. She admitted in interviews to having troubles with depression, self-harm, and eating disorders. She dated a series of bad men—most famously and destructively Blake Fielder-Civil, with whom she had a rather toxic on-again, off-again relationship. Winehouse, it seemed, wasn't able to take care of her body and was placed into a rehabilitation facility in order to have treatment for her anxiety, depression, and substance abuse. This would be the first of many trips for the singer to recover. None of them, it ultimately proved, helped her.

But despite all her personal troubles, the music lived within Amy Winehouse. In 2007, she began collaborating with music producer Mark Ronson, and they created the album *Back to Black*. The single "Rehab" was released just before the album, to tremendous acclaim. The song was meant to be tongue-in-cheek and perhaps even witty. Unfortunately, it would later prove to be a devastating reminder of the troubled singer's life. The album earned her seven Grammy awards, including "Best New Artist" for 2008, as well as "Song of the Year" and "Record of the Year." *Back to Black* was the seventh-highest-selling album of 2008. The subsequent tour began tremendously with sold-out concerts and much critical acclaim. But at a performance in November 2007, Winehouse was apparently drunk or high and was reduced to crying and stumbling around the stage in front of a booing and jeering audience.

Winehouse was in and out of rehab facilities over the following months, and she married long-time boyfriend Fielder-Civil, despite objections from both of their parents. People close to the families state that it was well known that the two of them harmed each other both emotionally and physically and that their relationship "revolved around drug use." Fielder-Civil even bragged to a British tabloid that he had introduced Winehouse to crack and heroin. But in 2008, Winehouse claimed "I literally woke up one day and was like, 'I don't want to do this anymore." She divorced Fielder-Civil in 2009, and by all accounts things were beginning to look up for the singer in her personal life, despite a few legal troubles and a few issues of public intoxication and violence. For, even though she had cut out illegal substances and a toxic husband, alcohol still continued to be a major influence in her life. Many photographs of Winehouse in various states of dress and inebriation began plaguing tabloids. Winehouse even went so far as to file an injunction against the paparazzi in 2009.

In the latter half of 2008, Winehouse was plagued with more health troubles, including emphysema, laryngitis, and an irregular heartbeat. But after some time in the hospital, agents for Winehouse reported that she was doing much better and would be recording a new album very soon. Over the next couple of years, she continued to work with some of the biggest names in music, including Questlove, Salaam Remi, Toni Bennett, and Ronson. She recorded several singles, mostly covers, including "It's My Party," and "You're Wondering Now." It seemed that, despite the singer's personal troubles, she was still known as one of the best artists to work with, and she had many projects in the works, including a song with Cee Lo Green, Janelle Monáe, and many others.

On July 23, 2011, Amy Winehouse was discovered by her bodyguard in her London apartment. He had spent the last three days checking on her diligently, as he felt she was a bit intoxicated. But on his final check up on the singer, he found her lying in bed, unable to be awakened. He immediately called for an ambulance. She was pronounced dead shortly after the paramedics arrived. The media was in a tizzy—reporting of a drug overdose, of suicide, and many other presumptions that would later prove untrue. Crowds of fans flocked to her apartment in the Camden neighborhood of London to pay their respects. Afterward, the singer broke a Guinness World Record—for a woman with the most singles to simultaneously appear on the UK's Billboard charts (eight).

Three empty bottles of vodka were discovered in the singer's apartment, and a toxicology report stated that Winehouse's blood alcohol content was 416 mg per 100 ml (0.416 percent), more than five times the legal limit when she died. Her death was ruled as "misadventure," due to accidental alcohol poisoning, although it was stated that the accidental alcohol poisoning was a result of her bulimia, which left her body weak and unable to process the alcohol.

Artists around the world have since paid their respects to the late singer: Bruno Mars, Nicki Minaj, Rihanna, Adele, George Michael, Lady Gaga, U2, M.I.A., Kelly Clarkson, and many more have dedicated songs to her. Punk rockers Patti Smith and Green Day both wrote songs for the late, great Amy Winehouse.

On what would have been the singer's thirty-first birthday, September 14, 2014, a statue was unveiled in Camden, London, where the singer lived. The bronze statue depicts the singer in her iconic look—with a large beehive, in a tight dress and her signature winged eyeliner. The sculptor, Scott Eaton, said the memorial was meant to capture her attitude, her strength, but also her insecurities.

Another life tragically cut short before its time, due to the influences of fame, and the dogged determination of the media to make a scandal out of anything. A troubled life, along with intense depression led to the substance abuse issues and eating disorder that claimed her life. But Amy Winehouse will live on in the hearts of fans and musicians alike. Her ability to blend the old with the new, to convey such raw emotion on stage, and to make her listeners feel everything she was feeling have cemented her among the ranks of the best musicians who ever lived. But it's clear even Amy Winehouse knew her star was going to burn out quickly, saying: "Life's short. Anything could happen, and it usually does, so there is no point in sitting around thinking about all the ifs, ands, and buts."

## Whitney Houston

Clive Davis, legendary music producer and record executive, throws a pre-Grammy party every year. It is the who's who of musicians, celebrities, and legends. In 2012, Whitney Houston, America's sweetheart, and the greatest voice of her generation, was scheduled to attend. She would never make it.

It had been a rough decade for Houston. The iconic singer who shot to fame in 1985 with a debut album that won her a Grammy had been in several cult-classic films including *The Bodyguard* (1993), which also produced one of her most famous songs, a cover of Dolly Parton's "I Will Always Love You," as well as *Waiting to Exhale, The Preacher's Wife*, and a made-for-TV

Superstar Whitney Houston and her daughter, Bobbi Kristina Brown, died under mysteriously similar circumstances.

rendition of Rogers and Hammerstein's *Cinderella* (which received critical acclaim for its all-star, ethnically diverse cast). But a very public divorce, rumors of drug abuse, a failed television show, and years out of the public eye had made Houston someone of a recluse as far as celebrities were concerned.

In 2009, Houston released her last album *I Look to You*. Fans and critics hoped that this would be the return of the Whitney they all loved. In 2010, she received a BET Honors Award for her twenty-five years in the industry. In 2011, Houston produced and starred alongside Jordin Sparks and Mike Epps in the film *Sparkle*. R and B singer Aaliyah originally had been slotted to star in the film, but the project was derailed after the star died in a plane crash in 2002. A single, "Celebrate," recorded with Houston and Aaliyah was released along with the film. Neither did spectacularly, but it was noted that Houston was trying to get herself, and her career, back on track.

On February 11, 2012, just hours before the Grammys, Houston was found dead in the bathtub of her hotel room in Beverly Hills. She was pronounced dead shortly after the paramedics arrived. A small spoon with a crystal-like substance and a rolled up piece of paper were found at the crime scene, along with an open bottle of champagne and several cigarette butts. Houston's driver's license and prescriptions were taken from the scene. Because she was found lying face down in the water, the corner declared that the singer died from a combination of drowning and effects of atherosclerotic heart disease (aggravated by the hot water and the steam in the bathroom) and cocaine use.

Just after her death, while the music world was still reeling, music's biggest night was to take place in Hollywood. The 54th Grammy Awards began with footage of Houston performing "I Will Always Love You" from the 1994 Grammys ceremony. This was followed with a prayer read by host LL Cool J. The "In Memoriam" tribute to stars who had died in the previous year happens during every Grammy ceremony. That year, the mon-

## Bobbi Kristina Brown (March 4, 1993 – July 26, 2015)

The only daughter of Whitney Houston and Bobby Brown, Bobbi Kristina grew up in the shadows of her parents' fame. In a tragic turn of events that closely mirrored her mother's death, Bobbi Kristina was found unconscious in the bathtub of her Georgia home on January 31, 2015. Her fiancé, Nick Gordon, attempted to resuscitate her. She was rushed to the hospital, but doctors were unable to revive her. She was kept on a medical ventilator and flown across the country to see specialists in Chicago by her father, to no avail. Bobbi Kristina died in hospice care on July 26, 2015, after a series of seizures rendered her brain-dead. She was just twenty-two years old.

The autopsy found no obvious signs of injury or underlying cause to her death. But rumors circulated that her fiancé was a gold digger and a murderer. Investigators found it more than a coincidence that Gordon was present for both Whitney Houston and Bobbi Kristina Brown's deaths. However, there were no bruises found on Bobbi Kristina's body, nor were there any drugs in her system, despite rumors that contradict these facts. Both women were found in bathtubs and were never able to be revived, despite medical experts' best attempts. A tragic coincidence? Or foul play?

tage was shown to Houston's recording of "Saving All My Love for You." Jennifer Hudson performed "I Will Always Love You," which brought the Grammy's telecast its second-highest ratings in history.

There was an invitation-only funeral service held at New Hope Baptist Church in Newark, New Jersey, on February 18, 2012. Stevie Wonder, Alicia Keys, and R. Kelley all performed, interspersed with choral hymns. Bobby Brown, Houston's ex-husband, was invited but decided not to attend.

Called the "Queen of Pop," Whitney Houston's death left a void in the music community. The circumstances surrounding her death are tragic, especially considering how hard she had worked her entire life to nurture her talent and to get back to the condition of her prime. Her voice is more than iconic—anyone who ever heard it couldn't deny its power and skill, and for many it still gives them goosebumps. Although her friends, family, and colleagues will forever miss her smile and her sparkle, her fans will forever miss her voice and the influence she had on music.

## The People *v.* Orenthal (O. J.) James Simpson

Orenthal James "The Juice" Simpson was one of the most famous men in America. An all-star running back who had won the Heisman Trophy in 1968, he went on to lead his NFL teams to victory after victory for eleven seasons. He was inducted into the Football Hall of Fame in 1983. In his quest for fame he appeared in many advertising campaigns and acted in TV and movies. Some of his most famous roles included Jernigan in *The Towering Inferno*, Kadi Touray in the original *Roots*, and Detective Nordberg in the *Naked Gun* trilogy.

He married Nicole Brown-Simpson in 1985, and the couple had two children. The family was the ultimate interracial power couple, attending Los Angeles parties and red-carpet events. Simpson was an American hero who had made it out of the projects, crossed racial lines, and was living the dream.

On June 12, 1994, the public got a very different idea of the kind of person O. J. Simpson was. Nicole Brown-Simpson, now divorced from O. J., and her friend Ron Goldman were discovered stabbed to death in Nicole's home on Bundy Drive, in the affluent neighborhood of Brentwood, California. There was blood everywhere. Nicole's head was nearly severed from her body. The primary piece of physical evidence discovered at the scene was a bloody black leather left-hand glove.

The star running back turned actor was immediately contacted by the police. Detectives went to his Rockingham estate in order to take care of the Simpson's two young children, who were in their mother's home at the time of the murder. Not finding O. J. at home, the detectives discovered a drop of blood on the handle of his white Ford Bronco. This gave them sufficient cause to enter the home. On the grounds, they discovered another bloody black leather glove—this one right-handed.

O. J. had left for Chicago on a red-eye flight the night of June 12. He returned the next day upon hearing about the murder of his ex-wife. And he was immediately put into handcuffs by police in front of his home—and in front of the media, who had already caught wind of the story. He was taken in for questioning and gave a sample of his blood. He had a couple of cuts on his hand, which he claimed he couldn't remember getting. He also had no real alibi for the time of the murder the night before, around 10 p.m. Although the murder weapon was never discovered, records showed that Simpson had purchased the type of weapon, a hunting knife, but Simpson no longer recalled where he had placed it. Bloody size 12 shoe prints that matched the treads of a pair of O. J.'s shoes were also found at the crime scene. Though still considered a suspect, O. J. was released.

On June 17, 1994, a warrant was issued for O. J.'s arrest. His lawyer, Robert Shapiro, expected O. J. to turn himself in.

But by 2 p.m., O. J. hadn't appeared, and the police issued an all points bulletin for the famous football player. At 5 p.m., Robert Kardashian, a friend of O. J.'s and one of his defense lawyers, read a letter penned by O.J. to the media, in which OJ described himself as a lost person: "First everyone understand I had nothing to do with Nicole's murder...Don't feel sorry for me. I've had a great life." Many interpreted this as a suicide note and, therefore, a quasi-confession of guilt.

But at around 6:30 p.m., a witness called the LAPD, claiming to have seen O. J. in his white Bronco. What followed was a slow-speed chase through the streets of Los Angeles, ending at OJ's home, Rockingham. The chase was plastered across every television in the nation, even interrupting coverage of the 1994 NBA finals. Inside the Bronco, police found a gun, $9,000 in cash, O. J.'s passport, and a fake beard. O. J. was taken into custody. On June 24, O. J. Simpson was arraigned, and he pleaded "not guilty." The trial of the century had begun.

For the next few months, the prosecution and the defense teams worked to build their cases, compile a jury, and prepare for a trial that they all knew would be a media frenzy. O. J. had enough money to hire the best lawyers in LA. Robert Shapiro and Johnnie Cochran led what was called the "Dream Team" of defense, while the prosecution was led by Marcia Clark and Christopher A. Darden for the people. The jury assembled was composed of eight African Americans, two Hispanics, one Caucasian, and one person of mixed race. A jury of mostly women, the prosecution had hoped to paint O. J. as a domestic abuser.

What the public didn't know about O. J. was that he had a history of domestic violence against Nicole. They had separated and reconciled several times over the course of their relationship. And Nicole had called 9-1-1 many times claiming abuse. There was even photographic evidence of Nicole's face, bruised and bloodied, after an assault. There had been eight separate instances of Nicole either filing charges or calling the police. The case had even been brought before a judge once before, Nicole claiming spousal abuse and O. J. pleading "no contest." One particularly damning piece of evidence was a recorded 9-1-1 call, revealed by the media, of Nicole calling for help while O. J. was apparently breaking into her house. "I think you know his record," she was heard saying, "He's gonna beat the sh** out of me."

Before her death, Nicole had even taken out a safety deposit box at a local bank. Inside, she placed photographs and

During O. J. Simpson's trial for the murder of Nicole Brown Simpson, he famously tried on ill-fitting gloves tied to the murder scene.

hospital records of her injuries, her will, and written accounts of the abuse. The prosecution called Denise Brown, Nicole's older sister, to testify. Brown stated that she remembered an event from 1982, twelve years before Nicole's death, when O. J. had thrown Nicole against a wall. It was looking more and more like O. J. Simpson had murdered his wife and her friend in a jealous, abusive rage.

And above all of this, the prosecution had their physical evidence. The bloody gloves that contained the DNA of both the Simpsons and Goldman. There was also a sock found in O. J.'s bedroom that had splatters of Nicole's blood and the bloody footprints and a trail of blood between Nicole's house and O. J.'s and DNA evidence of O. J.'s blood found at Nicole's house. The prosecution was confident that they not only had their man, but they also had their conviction.

But the "Dream Team" had a few tricks up their collective sleeves. First, the defense pointed out that there had been no history of abuse of Nicole by O. J. in the past five years. And then, they reminded the jury that O. J. did have an alibi of sorts—he claimed he was hitting golf balls in his yard at the time of the murder. They suggested that Nicole had recently begun a rather high-risk lifestyle of drug abuse, alcohol dependency, and hard partying, which may have led to a drug deal gone wrong. And then, they went after the LAPD.

This was just two years after the Rodney King riots in LA, in which a black man had been mercilessly beaten by white cops on the streets of Los Angeles, spurring a rash of riots in protest. Racial tension between the black community and the white officers policing them was at an all-time high. And so when Johnnie Cochran suggested that the police had mishandled the evidence they collected, suspicion grew among the jurors. Cochran suggested that police detectives, spurred by racism, had planted O. J.'s blood on the scene after they had collected it from him during questioning. The blood that had been collected, it was theorized, had been taken out of LAPD's crime lab to the scene at Rockingham. They showed videos of investigators collecting evidence from the crime scene in ways that didn't stand up to proper protocol.

The defense also suggested that the second bloody glove discovered at Rockingham by Detective Mark Fuhrman had been planted as well. Fuhrman had a reputation as a racist, renegade cop who tended to go especially hard on black suspects. But he had already testified, when questioned by the prosecution, that he was not a racist, had never used racial slurs, and performed his duties to the best of his abilities. But, an aspiring screenwriter had interviewed Fuhrman months before about his experiences on the force and had kept all of her recordings. The defense played these for the court, and the jury, along with the world, was appalled. Not only had Fuhrman been recorded saying derogatory remarks toward African Americans, but he had also repeatedly used a very offensive racial slur—over forty times on the tapes that were played. It was determined that Fuhrman had perjured himself on the stand.

And then, on June 15, 1995, almost six months into the trial, the defense proposed that O. J. try on the infamous black gloves. Without any hesitation, O. J. took the gloves and struggled to put them on over the latex gloves he was already wearing. They didn't fit. He held his hands up to the court as proof. The gloves, which had been the prosecution's main piece of evidence, didn't fit their suspect. In his closing argument, Johnnie Cochran famously said: "If it doesn't fit, you must acquit."

The trial lasted nearly nine months. The jury, sequestered for almost three months of that, was exhausted, and ready for the case to be over as much as anyone else was. There were fifty-eight witnesses called to the stand. 488 pieces of evidence were shown. And when the jury was finally sent to deliberate, they only took four hours to come back with a verdict of not guilty.

The nation was divided. Polls determined that many in the black community rejoiced at O. J.'s verdict, while many in the white community believed a guilty man had been set free. The most highly publicized murder trial in history was over. But was it a failure of the justice system or a failure of justice?

There has been much speculation about O. J.'s guilt or innocence. He has maintained that he did not kill his ex-wife. But he has been plagued with legal troubles since the trial. The state of California claims he owes nearly $2 million in back taxes. He lost his estate at Rockingham and was hammered with law suits from the Goldman family, as well as from a publisher with whom he signed a book deal but never delivered any work. In 2001, he was arrested for yanking the glasses off a motorist while driving in Miami. In 2002, he was arrested again for speeding through a protected manatee habitat. Finally, in 2007, O. J. was arrested for stealing sports memorabilia at gunpoint from a Las Vegas hotel room. He was found guilty of all charges and sentenced to thirty-three years in prison, with the possibility of parole in about nine (a possible release in 2017). O. J. Simpson is currently serving out his sentence at the Lovelock Correctional Center in Nevada as inmate number 1027820.

There have been countless documentaries, films, and books released about O. J. Simpson and his trial and endless speculation about whether or not he did it. One theory, only recently posited, suggests that O. J. may have indeed done it, but it wasn't necessarily his fault. Chronic traumatic encephalopathy (CTE) is commonly found in NFL players, who often receive severe head injuries while playing football. CTE is also referred to as "punch drunk," because it causes social instability, mood swings, erratic behavior, poor judgment, and an increased propensity for violence and criminal behavior. There are no tests for CTE, as it is still a newly discovered and widely misunderstood disease. But there have been many cases of pro athletes who have developed the condition. Many doctors, theorists, and fans suggest that O. J. may have CTE. His history of violence and legal troubles certainly seems to point to it.

Over twenty years after the murder, trial, and acquittal, O. J. Simpson has managed to stay in the limelight while purposefully maintaining a life outside of the public eye. There will always be questions about whether or not he murdered his ex-wife and her friend. We may never know if O. J. Simpson got away with murder, or if the media created a monster.

# Chapter Six: Secrets of the Past

## The Money Pit

The story of the money pit begins in 1795, when sixteen-year-old Daniel McGinnis paddled his canoe to Oak Island—so named because of the dense growth of mature oak trees that flourished across it. The island, crossed by a stretch of stagnant swampland, is just one of many in Mahone Bay, off the coast of Nova Scotia. The boy went ashore, gathered his picnic basket and rod, and moved inland to deposit them under the shade of one of the oaks. He found, in a small clearing, a gnarled old tree with the tell-tale grooves in its bark indicating where a block-and-tackle pulley system for hauling or lowering had been in place. Below the tree was a circular impression in the earth, an indentation that seemed to the boy as if a hole had been dug and then filled in rapidly. The replaced earth had not been stamped down hard enough to conceal all signs of digging. Daniel was convinced that he had hit on a clearing where buried treasure had been hidden away. After all, this was shortly after the days of pirates and turncoat brigadiers.

The boy forgot his fishing expedition and paddled back to the mainland to breathlessly tell his friends about what he had discovered. Gathering picks and shovels, he and friends Anthony Vaughan, thirteen, and John Smith, twenty, prepared for a return visit the following day.

Once they began to dig, they discovered McGinnis had been right. They found themselves burrowing down into some kind of chamber, the sides bearing pick and shovel marks from long ago. When they had gone down just over ten feet (three meters) they struck a smooth-faced flagstone. Scraping away across the floor of the pit they realized that they had discovered an entire floor of such stones. Underneath, they dreamed, must be the treasure. But when the heavy stones were pried from the clay, there was nothing but more earth. Over the course of the following week they continued digging and at 20 feet (6 m), and 30 feet (9.1 m) they hit a flooring of closely packed oak logs. They also discovered a layer of coconut fibers. The disillusioned but intrigued youngsters decided to abandon their venture. In the way of all excited young men, they pledged an oath to return. And unlike most of these hastily made and hastily broken pledges, one of them kept their word, returning to the island nine years later for a more thorough, scientific excavation of the pit. Nothing had dented John Smith's certain knowledge that deep in the shaft lay treasure. Smith secured the financial backing of a syndicate, comprised of local businessmen, but funded chiefly by Simeon Lynds. When they got back to Oak Island the shaft looked much as they had left it all those years before. Using the money from the syndicate, a workforce was raised among local farm laborers and work began in earnest, digging deeper and deeper toward the glittering prize, which Smith knew was there. At 40 feet (12.19 m), they discovered a layer of coal. At 50 and 60 feet (15.24 and 18.28 m), they discovered a layer of coconut fibers and putty. Then, at 90 feet (27.43 m), something even stranger was dug up from the pit. A stone—not of indigenous Nova Scotia rock—that bore an inscription in a language no one had ever encountered before. Smith, a successful businessman in his own right by then, had actually purchased the whole island. He took the stone and put it over his hearth, the significance, if any, of the almost illegible script completely lost on him.

After the stone was wrenched free, another layer of wood lay underneath. Finally, although there was no reason to suggest why, the syndicate thought that under this wood lay the caskets of treasure. They resolved to rest for the night for a final surge in the morning that would make them wealthy. They were all of the mind that twenty-four hours would not make any difference.

In fact the men left the pit for forty-eight hours (the following day was Sunday, and Smith declared no work on the Sabbath). On Monday morning the men returned to the pit to find it flooded almost to the top. They frantically began bailing using an outmoded pump bought by the syndicate from an old oilfield. Their efforts were in vain—no matter how hard they pumped or how furiously they bailed, the water stayed a constant level below the lip of the shaft entrance. It was defeat bitter enough to make them abandon the shaft for a year.

The following spring they hit upon a new idea; burrowing a separate shaft alongside the original. Then they planned to break through and release the water into the surplus pit and then resume work on the treasure hunt. All went well until the final stages when the walls of the new hole suddenly caved in, hurling tons of water and earth on to the diggers. They were lucky to escape. That pit also flooded to the same level as the first. Smith and his partners finally conceded defeat to the forces of nature, reasoning that an underground spring lay beneath the site that had such force that they were never likely to reach their goal.

The next attempt to discover the secrets of the money pit came in 1849, when a new consortium of wealthy businessmen was formed. Called The Truro Syndicate (taking their name from the Cornwall district once rich in tin mines) they included in their ranks Anthony Vaughan, who had once again become intrigued by the treasure island he first dug on all those years ago. Dr. David Lynds, a relative of Simeon Lynds, was also one of the backers.

The first shaft was drained using more modern, powerful pumps and cleared out completely. There seemed to be no

Fortune hunters have searched for the money pit on Oak Island, Nova Scotia, for decades, with no success.

problem clearing out water or debris from the caved-in second shaft. But again, after calling a halt on Saturday night and returning on Monday morning, the syndicate found that the shaft was completely flooded. After several more pumping and bailing methods, the syndicate decided to use a drill that was driven by a horse. This would bore through the different layers below. Borings from the drill produced clay, gravel, mud, and sand. To the east of the pit, at a depth of over 100 feet (32 m), they discovered fragments of oak, pieces of metal, more oak, and finally a bed of spruce needles before finally hitting the clay bed again. A faint jarring motion on the drill as it went down made the searchers believe they had brushed past two treasure chests.

Next occurred one of those puzzling episodes for which a completely satisfactory answer has never been found. The drilling foreman, James Pitblado, was accused by one of the tough laborers of taking something shiny from the drill after it was brought to the surface. The laborer who witnessed this incited the other men to believe Pitblado had pocketed a jewel of some kind, and they demanded that he produce the gem at a meeting. Pitblado refused, saying he would announce his discovery, whatever it may have been, to the directors of the syndicate the next time a meeting was held. Pitblado then tried to buy the entire eastern end of Oak Island, away from the money pit. He was unsuccessful in his venture and vanished shortly afterward— the riddle of what he pocketed still unanswered.

In 1850 a new shaft was dug. That too flooded. But this time a curious laborer tasted the water on his hands. He was curious about the popular underground-stream theory because the heavy clay, like that on his farm, was impervious to water. Tasting the water gave the searchers the clue they were seeking about the flooding pit—it was seawater. On a nearby beach the syndicate unearthed another of the amazing secrets of the money pit.

"As the tide receded the sand seemed to suck the water down, like it was thirsty," noted one syndicate member, James Jolton. They excavated the sand to discover a truly remarkable engineering feat. Whoever had originally dug the money pit had ensured its safety by an intricate system designed to flood it if intruders came close to penetrating its secrets. A tunnel of stones, sealed over with kelp grass and coconut fiber, led in a slanting direction from the beach to the money pit. The grass and fiber kept out sand, which would have clogged the tunnel but allowed the water to run freely through it. The stone tunnel led straight back to the pit, entering the shaft at a depth of 98 feet (30 m). As long as the pit stayed full of earth, the water would be kept out. But as soon as the diggers reached it, the water burst through as high tide was reached, keeping the secrets of the pit safe. Smith had not been beaten by nature, but by a carefully designed and built man-made security system.

At first the prospectors tried damming the tunnel, a solution that failed when it was smashed by an unusually high tide. Then they tried to block the tunnel completely by digging yet another shaft near to the site of the original. Water flooded in at a depth of just under 36 feet (11 m) after the laborers had dislodged a boulder. The party thought they had intercepted the tunnel from the beach, but they were not deep enough. Wood was driven into the soft earth to stem the flow of the water and yet another shaft was dug. At 118 feet (36 m) they tunneled sideways into the original shaft and the whole thing collapsed. Miraculously no one was injured. Another nine years passed before the syndicate returned— but again with no success. More shafts were sunk and flooded. It was then that the money pit claimed its first victim: a worker scalded to death when a steam pump blew.

After the Truro Syndicate abandoned its operations, hopeful treasure hunters spurred on by the lure of great wealth arrived like locusts on the island. Soon the area around the pit resembled a pock-marked moon surface with countless shafts and holes. One man even attempted to swim to the bottom of the flooded original shaft using primitive diving apparatus!

In 1891 the search was passed on to the Oak Island Treasure Company, which was headed by Frederick Leander Blair. He organized one assault on the original shaft, but when that failed, the pit lay dormant for six years as the syndicate struggled to raise more money. It wasn't until 1897 that the excavation began again at the mouth of the flood tunnel. Nearly 154 pounds (70 k) of dynamite was lowered into the mouth of the tunnel and detonated to prevent further flooding. They drained the pit, came back the next day and found it flooded again! Then, using a drill encased in piping to ensure smoother operating, a bore was lowered into the murky depths. At 124 feet (38 m) it bit into a sheet of iron. A smaller drill was passed down and this drilled through the obstruction to a depth of 150 feet (46 m), passing en-route through some soft stone. Twenty inches (53 cm) below that it hit some oak, then hit more metal, and a fragment of parchment. When the parchment was examined on the surface it contained the letters V. I. When the engineers attempted to insert piping down the length of the drill to obtain further samples, the bit was deflected, and water rushed up the bore pipe at enormous pressure. Blair, thinking that he had struck yet another water barrier that the ingenious mind behind the construction of the pit had devised, poured in red dye and ordered laborers to watch the sea. Sure enough, red dye seeped into the sea in three different areas, confirming more water barriers constructed to keep the pit from the reach of man. The syndicate sunk fourteen more shafts in a bid to block the tunnels, failing in their plan and turning the area around the pit into a maze of holes and swamps. The syndicate bankrupted itself soon after.

The next plan came in 1909, when rich engineer Captain Henry Bowdoin invested in a new drill. He failed. Then in 1912 a scientist tried a scheme to freeze all the water in the pit and hack it out with picks. He too failed. For the next twenty years the D-I-Y prospectors picked over the ravaged site, the original shaft barely discernible from the countless other pits and holes that dotted the area. In the 1930s several schemes were formulated by wealthy businessmen. One involved rigging up a system of steel pylons ringing the site to keep out the water, another sending divers in a diving bell to the water's depths. Only one explorer distinguished himself from the others with their madcap schemes—an adventurer called Gilbert Hedden, who found a large triangular pile of stones on a deserted beach near to where the original tunnel was located. There was also an arrow pointed toward where the money pit lay. Hedden, using a chart he claimed was printed in a book called *Captain Kidd and his Skeleton Island*, which chronicled the exploits of one of history's most infamous pirates, said his discovery proved conclusively that the treasure was the property of the infamous pirate. While many subscribed to Hedden's theory, others poured scorn on it.

Hedden was followed by engineer Edwin Hamilton, who drilled the deepest shaft of 180 feet (53 m) and discovered that the second tunnel entered the pit at 150 feet (46 m) on the opposite of the original flood tunnel. In 1963 the next casualties of the mystifying hole occurred when on August 17, Robert Restall was overcome by the exhaust fumes of his water pump, killing him, his father, and two other men who tried to rescue them. In 1965, a geologist, Robert Dunfield, squandered £120,000 (roughly $915,184 today) in digging more new holes, without any success.

To this day the secrets of the money pit have not been penetrated. In 2014, Rick and Marty Lagina, two brothers from Michigan, began a new effort to discover the secrets held by the money pit. Funded by the History Channel, their efforts have been documented by film crews and have created three seasons of the show *The Curse of Oak Island.* So far, even with all of their funding, high-tech equipment,mworkers, experts, and support from the outside, the brothers have yet to yield any more evidence than any of their predecessors.

Whoever built the money pit, and whatever secrets it holds, whether it is treasure, secret documents, or a secret entrance to a lost city, the secret lies intact in the mud and clay of that lonely little island.

## Secrets of the Standing Stones

They stand as mighty symbols of a time that modern man barely comprehends. The scant knowledge gleaned of the ages when the massive stones were formed has been unearthed through archaeological studies and examination of artifacts left behind. No records exist to tell us what made the ancient inhabitants of Salisbury plain build the circling stones that are the enduring legacy of not-so-primitive man. And no pot, pan, or flint head, valuable though they are, can express the brooding, dark secrets of that age when the most famous of all the megaliths that span Western Europe was constructed. Centuries on, the giants of Stonehenge still keep their secrets.

The ancient monument itself is but one of a number of "megaliths," Greek for "great stones," that cut across Europe in a giant swathe. There are sites in Brittany, Malta, and Spain, and nine hundred in the British Isles alone, the northernmost ones situated on the windswept Shetland Isles. But Stonehenge has come to symbolize the age of the megaliths, with all its sinister and mysterious connotations of human sacrifice, sun worship, and pagan rituals. The monument itself was built in three distinct phases spanning a period of over 1,300 years. Each group that embarked on the mammoth task of hauling, carving, and placing the stones did not quite manage to complete their work— leaving the job to be finished by their successors.

Historians agree that the first builders were neolithic, beginning the original construction around 2700 B.C. These first hunter-warriors excavated the encircling ditch and erected the so-called heel stone, which is aligned so that the first rays of light from the sun on Midsummer's Day strike it and the central point of the inner stone circle. The same men dug the Aubrey Holes; the fifty-six shallow pits which form a ring near the banked earth surrounding the structure at Stonehenge. When the pits were excavated earlier this century they contained a wealth of burned objects and charred bones, giving rise to one theory that the stones constituted a holy cremation ground for early man. Eight hundred and fifty years after man began the first steps toward creating Stonehenge, the race called the Beaker people moved in to finish the massive stone legacy. The Beaker people, whose name derived from their habit of burying their dead with ornate pots and vases, accomplished amazing engineering feats that have baffled and bemused modern technicians. Theirs is truly one of the great secrets of Stonehenge. For the Beaker people, equipped with flint head axes and without the use of the wheel, quarried rock from Wales and dragged it to Stonehenge! Over 300 miles (480 km) from the hills of South Wales, to the plateau of Stonehenge, were dragged the enormous stones; eighty in all, each weighing more than four tons, the stones were assembled into a double circle. This is an accomplishment that modern researchers have yet to figure out.

No less impressive a feat occurred around 1500 BCE when the Beaker people, who failed in their bid to finish the construction, were themselves succeeded by another unnamed generation, who harnessed the labor of an estimated one thousand workers or slaves to drag quarried stones from the downs near modern-day Marlborough to the Stonehenge

Mysteries surround the origins of the prehistoric monument Stonehenge, located in England.

site. Historians can only concur that primitive sledges were used to haul the stones in an operation that would have taken months to complete. Once at the site, they were fashioned into the giant stones that exist as the Stonehenge we know. And these same craftsmen, who had devised no system that we know of to read, write, or perform mathematics, created a system to lever into place the giant lintels which crown the upright stones. The means by which they did this is unknown, but Stonehenge man shared something in common with his fellow megalith builders in Europe and other parts of the British Isles; all the monuments are constructed using the same unit of measurement, which has since become known as the Megalith Yard, a distance of 2 feet (.83 m). How or why this common unit of measurement came to be used by these "primitive" people is something that has not been satisfactorily explained.

The cult of druidism is espoused by the heirs to the ancient Celtic priests, who lay claim to Stonehenge and each summer solstice are allowed access to the well-guarded national monument to practice their ancient rites. But experts concur that it is too old to have been built by their forefathers, the original druids.

The most widely accepted theory about the origins and construction of Stonehenge is that propounded by Oxford University professor Alexander Thom, who after long days sailing on Loch Roag on the Isle of Lewis, off Scotland's bleak western coastline, stopped to gaze at the standing stones of Callanish, often dubbed "Scotland's Stonehenge." He went ashore, and standing in the center of the stones, checked the position of the pole star. He was able to determine that the structure was aligned due north-south. But because this monument was prehistoric, and was built in a time when the pole star's constellation had not reached its present position in the galaxy, Professor Thom reasoned that its architects must have had some other means of determining the alignment of the stones. Excited by his discovery, Professor Thom embarked on a journey throughout Britain and Europe to examine more than six hundred standing stone sites. And they all proved his theory was correct—that the stones were, in fact, crude space observatories. All were built on the north-south axis, marking the moments throughout the calendar when the sun and moon rose and set.

In 1963, Gerald Hawkins, professor of astronomy at Boston University, took the Thom theory one step farther and announced that Stonehenge was, in fact, a massive prehistoric computer, capable of complex calculations based on the heavens. "The men that built it proved they were not primitive by dint of their architecture," he said. The published works of C. A. Newham followed on by stating that a caste of highly evolved astronomer-priests would have stood in the centre of the stones and tracked the path of the sun and moon by using the stones as a guide. Euan Mackie of Glasgow's Hunterian Museum took the elite caste system theory farther when he announced that he had found the stone age "university" where these priests may have lived and trained. Artifacts of woven cloth, remains of a rich diet, and other objects found at Durrington Walls near Stonehenge were proof of a higher quality of life among a select few that distinguished them from their fellow men.

If what the academics say is true, then the widely held belief that Stonehenge was a place of pagan worship is inaccurate. It also means that, in a time when there was no numeracy or literacy, an intellectual elite existed within the stone age communities and, somehow, gleaned the knowledge to measure the Megalithic Yard and to chart planetary movements. Professor Sir Fred Hoyle, one of Britain's foremost astronomers, also supported the theory that Stonehenge was a giant observatory. He agreed with Hawkins's speculation that the stones could be used as markers to gauge the moon's activity as it passed through its lunar cycle. The Aubrey Holes, dug by the first workers on the site, were significant, said Hoyle; their number, fifty-six, representing almost exactly three times the 18.6 years of the moon's cycle. When he fed this into a computer he found out that the stones could predict eclipses of the sun! "The construction demanded a level of intellectual attainment greater than the standard to be expected from a 'primitive' community," he said.

As to other theories about the mysterious stones, the enthusiast for mystery can choose any one of a number: that the site was a marker for aliens from outer space to land their craft; that it was a place where infertile women went to be blessed; that it was a temple for human sacrifice, an altar to the gods who saw over the harvest, or a forum for a primitive parliament.

Only those massive, immoveable stones know the true history of Stonehenge—and they cannot reveal their secrets. It's up to archaeologists, researchers, and inquisitive minds to find out the answers.

## Secret Societies

Conspiracy theorists, historians, and experts agree: secret societies have been a part of the country for as long as can be remembered. From Skull and Bones, to the Rosicrucians, the Knights Templar, and the Illuminati, human history is littered with these secret societies that, if rumors are true, have forever altered culture.

### The KKK

Of all the world's secret societies that have their origins in the past, few are more hated than the dreaded Ku Klux Klan. Founded on Christmas Eve 1865 by former Confederate general Nathan Forrest and five other Civil War veterans in Pulaski, Tennessee, the Klan was originally formed to stop the "Yankee" carpetbaggers from taking over what remained of the ruined south.

However, the purpose of this "organization" quickly changed as white southerners had difficulty adjusting to their lives as former slave owners and their prejudiced beliefs brought their racism to a boil. The general and his friends gave themselves preposterous titles, such as "Imperial Wizard," and dressed themselves in white hooded robes to shield their identities.

Within two years, the group, which by now comprised hundreds of former slave owners and soldiers, was waging an all-out terror campaign against blacks across the southern states of America. Intimidation of Jews and Catholics was soon to follow. Using violence and threats, the KKK played a key role in shaping the beliefs and customs of the postwar Deep South, using its considerable clout to influence elections and derail any legislation it considered detrimental to its aim of total white supremacy. The KKK also murdered on a huge scale without fear of ever being caught, largely because no one knew the identities of the members, and those who did were sworn to secrecy. The penalty for breaking the Klan code of silence was death.

According to historians, more than 3,500 African-American men, women, and children were murdered in the Klan's first ten years of existence, as the shadowy organization spread its tentacles further and further across the defeated and demoralized southern states.

By the 1920s, at the height of its popularity, the Klan had about five million members, including doctors, lawyers, police officers, judges, and other pillars of white society. Even the so-called "liberal" northern states fell victim to the scourge, as Klan groups appeared in industrial cities like St. Louis, Chicago, New York, Baltimore, and Washington, DC, where there were a dwindling number of jobs and increasing local resentment for the number of immigrant workers. The Klan's burning crosses and hateful rhetoric struck fear in minority groups across the nation, and more than nine hundred African Americans alone were lynched in the decade.

The Ku Klux Klan has publicly terrorized minority groups for much of America's history, but membership is a tightly-held secret.

During the 1960s, the Klan was also at the forefront of attacks on civil rights groups at a time when southern states were ordered by the federal government to desegregate their schools, hotels, stores, and restaurants. Claiming they were trying to protect "the old way of life," the KKK embarked on a campaign to block the inevitable changes in civil rights. They lynched local blacks, bombed churches, and burned down minority-owned farms and businesses. In 1964, Klansmen brazenly killed three civil rights workers as they drove across Mississippi trying to rally support for their cause.

As civil rights in the United States have improved over the years, membership in the Klan has dwindled. The latest government data estimates put the number of Klansmen at about eight thousand, with two-thirds estimated to be located in the South, and the other third in the Midwest. However, the KKK still has not forsaken its violent tactics. Its members still attack black families, peace activists, and Jewish communities, and as recently as 1981 the Klan lynched a teenage black man.

Of most concern today to law enforcement groups and civil liberty organizations is the growing alliance between the KKK and the neo-Nazi movement. According to FBI reports, neo-Nazi attacks on minority groups have more than tripled in the past two years, and the group has been blamed for several racially-motivated murders. In 1995, Don Black and Chloê Hardin, former KKK grand wizard David Duke's ex-wife, created the website Stormfront, which has become an online gathering place for white supremacist, neo-Nazism, racism, and hate speech in general.

The thugs, who have become virtual storm troopers for the older Klansmen, were brought into the racist fold by Tom Metzger, a longtime KKK operative and avowed white supremacist. The neo-Nazis act as bodyguards at Klan rallies and gained national notoriety when they started a studio brawl on a television show that was probing the reemergence of hate groups in the United States.

The white-robed Klansmen are a dark a blot on society. Together with their neo-Nazi comrades, they have spread their campaign in recent years to include international recruitment and to spread hate speech against homosexuals, Muslims, and immigrants. They blame all episodes of urban violence upon the "mixed race population" of large cities, specifically the Muslim, Latino, and black communities. Some KKK groups are becoming more and more integrated with their neo-Nazi brethren and have adopted the look of white supremacist skinheads—shaving their heads and tattooing their bodies with swastikas and other symbols of racism.

A person must be approached in order to join the organization, and one can only imagine what sort of actions it takes to get their attention. It is hard to determine how, or when, a society such as this will stop threatening other citizens of their nations. And while their identities remain a secret, their cause does not.

## The Mafia

From its humble beginnings many, many years ago in the small towns and villages of Sicily and southern Italy, the Mafia is probably the most feared and dangerous secret organization in the world. During its incredibly violent history, it has carved out a multibillion-dollar criminal empire dwarfing even the assets of the largest legitimate corporations, protecting its ill-gotten gains with murder, bribery, extortion, and a code of silence: the *omerta*, which if broken is punishable by death.

Few men have ever lived to break the omerta, but in 1985, Tommaso Buscetta, a Mafia chief, revealed to a hushed New York courtroom the most secret rituals of the underworld crime tzars. "I was given a 'saint' [a wallet-size picture of a saint with a small prayer printed underneath] and then my finger was pricked and I had to rub blood from my finger onto the saint and then set fire to it and I had to say the oath. After...I was to say that if I should betray the organization, my flesh would burn like this saint." Buscetta also revealed that the mobsters regard themselves as "men of honor," who are sworn under penalty of death not to touch another mafioso's wife or lie to another member.

According to law enforcement officials, the Mafia, or "Cosa Nostra" (Italian for "This Thing of Ours"), is made up of just a few thousand members, but has tens of thousands of associates. The Mafia gained a foothold in the United States when Italian immigrants arrived en masse during the early 1900s. In run-down neighborhoods of cities like New York and Chicago, young packs of hoodlums would extort money from their hardworking countrymen.

The rise of the Mafia, in the form we know it today, began with the murder of one of the first major syndicate bosses, Nicholas Morello, leader of the Sicilian gangsters in New York, who was shot to death in September 1917. Following his execution, the two warring Mafia factions, those of Sicilian and Neapolitan descent, merged for the first time and operated under the leadership of Guiseppe "Joe the Boss" Masseria for nearly a decade. Eventually, Masseria was executed by one of his top henchmen who, just five months later, was himself killed. The next day, forty old Mafia mobsters were murdered by killers loyal to a "rising star" on the Mafia scene, Charles "Lucky" Luciano, the man credited with establishing the Mafia "family" system in the United States.

Luciano carved New York City up into five criminal families, all headed by men he could trust—other cities across the nation soon followed suit. Within a decade, Luciano was known as the "Capo di tutti Capi," Boss of All Bosses, and the first Mafia godfather. He also created "the commission"—a mob board of directors made up from the heads of the families which decided who could become members of the clan, which family got what share of business, and when another mobster had to be executed.

The Prohibition years of the 1920s and early 1930s fueled the mob's financial coffers and political clout, as the nation turned to the bootleggers for its booze. Thugs like Al Capone and Frank Nitty rose to incredible heights of power during those violent days, when the Mafia families virtually controlled the cities in which they were based. It was said that Capone ruled every senior politician, judge, and police officer in Chicago during Prohibition.

After Congress repealed Prohibition in 1933, the Mafia began to look to new ways of making money and quickly became more involved in drugs and gambling. Las Vegas, it has been said, was built by mob money.

During the 1940s, 1950s, and 1960s, scores of mobsters were ordered to be "taken out" by rival gangsters as the battles for new sources of revenue heated up across the country. Leadership succession was shaped to a large degree by assassinations. One of the most ruthless hit men of the period was Albert Anastasia, who headed the infamous "Murder Incorporated," which hired itself out to whoever could afford the special services it offered. Anastasia, like many of his peers, was himself eventually murdered.

He was shot to death in October 1957, while he sat in the barber shop of a New York hotel.

Although the family system of Mafia rule has survived to the present day, federal prosecutors and law enforcement officials have scored successes against the organization. However, authorities predict a new breed of leaders will soon emerge and fear a new wave of battles, as mobsters fight for power.

In 1992, John Gotti, the last remaining Mafia boss, was convicted of conspiracy to commit murder, racketeering, obstruction of justice, illegal gambling, extortion, tax evasion, and loansharking. He was sentenced to life in prison. The FBI had their sights on Gotti for many years, but it was the testimony of his second in command, Salvatore "Sammy the Bull" Gravano, which gave sufficient evidence to convict the criminal. He died of throat cancer in June of 2002, while still in prison. His conviction, according to other members of the Mafia, was considered the end of the American Mafia.

The Mafia no longer has the control over businesses and government in the United States it once did. However, that does not mean it has been eliminated. The FBI still keeps watch on some of the oldest Mafia families. And it is impossible to tell exactly how many crime lords and underlings still have their fingers in the black market economy. Although their numbers have dwindled, there's no doubt they have old money, old power, and old connections. And one thing is for certain—they are absolutely still feared.

## The Masons

Not all the world's secret societies are committed to crime, violence, or other forms of chaos and intimidation. In fact, one of the oldest and largest of the secret groups, the Freemasons, was originally formed to protect the professional and religious interests of a particular group of craftsmen: stonemasons.

Despite what some masons may proclaim, however, the beginnings of Freemasonry do not go back to the biblical days of King Solomon. On the contrary, the organization was founded in London in 1717 at the Goose and Gridiron Tavern. Throughout the previous century, membership in guilds of men actually working as stonemasons began to decline rapidly. To bolster their dwindling membership, the masons opened their doors to honorary members, who became known as Freemasons.

The exact origin of the name "Freemason" is shrouded in mystery, although it has been in use for several centuries. Some scholars believe the word stems from the fact that masons were free from feudal serfdom, while others believe it points to a worker who fashioned freestone. Regardless, within sixteen years, borrowing rituals and symbols from many ancient sources, the number of Freemason lodges had grown to 126, and soon the secret order of the brotherhood was spreading throughout Europe and the new world. In fact, Freemasonry became so acceptable in the United States, that there is ample evidence to suggest that it was a highly influential force in framing the constitution, even in designing the Great Seal of the United States, which is full of masonic symbols such as the all-seeing eye set within a triangle and the unfinished pyramid, which represents the unfinished temple of Solomon.

In recent years, however, the Freemasons or "brotherhood," as they are sometimes known, have received a certain amount of criticism. This has arisen from growing suspicion about the continued intense secrecy surrounding the society's rituals and aims and a feeling that Freemasons may put the interests of the society and their fellow members before that of say, the organization they work for. For instance, there have been recommendations by a number of senior police chiefs that policemen should not be members of any masonic lodge as this could present them with a conflict of interest in the course of their police work.

To become a Freemason, a candidate must undergo a series of highly secret ceremonies and tests. If an applicant is accepted by the lodge (it must be by unanimous vote), he must submit himself to the three degree rituals which promote him among the organization.

First, his head is covered and he is stripped to his underwear and undershirt. He is made to repeat numerous, often bizarre oaths. For the first degree of membership, "the Entered Apprentice," the applicant's left breast, shoulder, and arm are then bared and a rope is tied around his neck. For the second degree of membership, "the Fellow Craft," the man's right breast, shoulder, and arm are exposed. The rope is tied around his upper right arm. The third or "Master Mason" degree also requires the candidate to be disrobed and blindfolded. The rope is then placed around the man's body three times.

In all three instances, the candidate must go through this procedure before he takes the oath for each degree. The Master Mason obligation, for instance, offers a blood-curdling penalty for violating the oath and failing in one's duties. It reads, in part, that a candidate "will promise and swear that I will not write, print, stamp, stain, hew, cut, carve, indent, paint ,or engrave (masonic secrets) ... binding myself under no less penalty than to have my throat cut across, my tongue tom out by the roots, and my body buried in the rough sands of the sea at low water mark."

Freemasonry, if nothing else, has a sense of the dramatic, but members insist it is a just society with secrets, not a secret society. But of all the fraternal groups, Freemasons see the rituals and rites of their brotherhood as the essence of the organization's very being.

## The Man in the Iron Mask

The great novelist Alexandre Dumas immortalized him in his novel of the same name—the story of the wretch kept imprisoned in a mask of iron, his identity shielded from the world, the secret of his crime lodged only with the king and perhaps a few of his trusted advisers. He wore the mask for thirty years, ate with it on, slept with it on. Even at his death the contraption stayed on his face. Who was he? What was the secret of his crime? It is a mystery that has endured to this day with many theories put forward but few concrete answers.

It was on the personal command of the Sun King, Louis XIV of France, builder of the great Palace of Versailles, that the identity of the man in the iron mask was kept secret—not only from his subjects, but from his court and the jailers. For three decades he lived in solitary confinement in different prisons, ending his days in France's most infamous jail, the Bastille. When he died in 1703, the furniture in his cell was burned, the whitewash on the walls was repainted to erase any pathetic attempt he might have made at an epitaph to the world, and the metalwork of his mask was melted down. Those who had kept his identity secret in life were determined that he should remain anonymous even when he was dead.

It was not until fifty years after his death that historians began to probe into the identity of this strange man and to discover what his crime had been. First, a journal containing an entry describing the man's death surfaced in Paris.

Up until the French Revolution in 1789, it was presumed that only de Saint-Mars and the king knew the identity of the prisoner. It was certainly not passed on within the House of Bourbon, for neither of Louis's successors knew who he was. The last king of France, Louis XVI, began a frantic search for it at the request of his wife, Marie Antoinette.

When the French Revolution overturned Europe's established order in a tidal wave of change, numerous government agencies were ransacked by rising politicians such as Maximilian Robespierre. Often the aim was to find information valuable for their own ends; however, papers found in the minister of war's office in Paris shed intriguing light on the secret of France's most celebrated captive. It transpired that for years de Saint-Mars had corresponded with a man named Louvois, a functionary of some kind in the prison service. In July 1669, Louvois wrote to de Saint-Mars: "The King has commanded that I am to have the man named Eustache Dauger sent to Pignerol. It is of the utmost importance to his service that he should be most securely guarded and that he should in no way give information about himself nor send letters to anyone at all. You will yourself, once a day, have to take enough food for the day to this wretch and you must on no account listen for any reason at all to what he may want to say to you, always threatening to kill him if he opens his mouth to speak of anything but his necessities."

During the reign of seventeenth-century French king Louis XIV, a mysterious figure known as the Man in the Iron mask was held prisoner.

Then another letter, from the king himself, was also unearthed in the war minister's archives, written to de Saint-Mars, which said: "I am sending to my citadel of Pignerol, in the charge of Captain de Vauroy, sergeant major of my city and citadel of Dunkirk, the man named Eustache Dauger. You are to hold him in good and safe custody; prevent him from communicating with anyone at all, by word of mouth or writ of hand. So be it."

Up until the discovery of these letters, it was widely believed that the false name he was buried under, Marchioly, was a bastardization of Mattioli, an envoy of the duke of Mantua who had once incurred the king's wrath. Mattioli did indeed end up in penal servitude in Pignerol, but he and the man in the iron mask were two very separate people.

Nineteenth century research into Eustache Dauger proved this: he was one of six brothers, four of whom fell in battle. He came from the northern French fishing port of Dunkirk and was believed at one time to have been a lieutenant in the elite King's Guards, a feat made possible by virtue of his brother's elevation to the nobility.

With his brother circulating in court circles, and himself guarding the heart of the realm, Eustache came close to the wicked Madame de Montespan, the king's mistress and a dabbler in black magic. Those close to the royal circle knew that de Montespan was strong medicine for the king, and that he tolerated her heretical indulgences because he was fascinated by her and, some say, in love with her. It is possible, therefore, that Eustache Dauger became entranced by her, went to a black mass, and was discovered by the king. He could not have him spreading the word that the king's concubine indulged in devil worship. Perhaps that was the reason for the years in jail. Perhaps the king was merely jealous, paranoid that a mere soldier was set to steal his sweetheart from him. But why not have him executed? Louis was, after all, a monarch with absolute power.

To this day the secret of the man in the iron mask remains as steadfast as the forged metal that kept his face from the world for over thirty years. But one thing is certain—this enigma has fascinated people for nearly three hundred years. And that fascination will not fade until the mystery is solved.

# GLOSSARY

**abdicate**—To formally renounce the throne.

**bore**—To dig a deep hole, especially with a cylindrical tool.

**carpetbagger**— A political candidate who seeks election in an area where they have no local connections or affiliations.

**caste**— A social class.

**communism**—A political theory created by Karl Marx in which all property is controlled by the government and goods are doled out according to public needs.

**dinghy**— A small rowboat for recreational use.

**fascism**—An authoritarian and nationalistic idealistic form of government and political order.

**fatwa**— A ruling in Islamic law given by an authority figure.

**immunity**— To be legally released from any responsibility for crimes in exchange for information that leads to the arrest of a larger criminal.

**indicted**— To formally accuse or charge with a serious crime.

**lynching**—To hang someone by the neck until dead unlawfully.

**modus operandi**— The way in which a criminal commits his crime; the signatures which they place on their crimes.

**neo-Nazi**— a member of the new Nazi party, which believes many of the Third Reich's teachings.

**numeracy**— Knowledge of numbers and arithmetic.

**prosecution**—The institution in charge of legal proceedings against a person accused of a crime.

**subpoenaed**—A written document legally ordering a person to appear in court or give up evidence for the court.

**supremacist**—A person (or persons) who is extreme in his or her specific set of beliefs.

# FURTHER READING

## Books

Greenberg, Andy. *This Machine Kills Secrets: Julian Assange, the Cypherpunks, and Their Fight to Empower Whistleblowers.* New York, NY: Dutton, 2012.

Leaming, Barbara. *Marilyn Monroe.* New York, NY: Three Rivers Press, 2000.

Owen, Mark. *No Easy Day: The Firsthand Account of the Mission that Killed Osama bin Laden.* New York, NY: Dutton, 2012.

Riley, Mike. *More Hollywood Murders and Scandals: Tinsel Town After Dark,* Las Vegas, NV: Maica International LLC, 2014.

Riley, Mike. *Murders Unsolved: Cases That Have Baffled The Authorities For Years,* Las Vegas, NV: Maica International LLC, 2014.

Shepard, Geoff. *The Real Watergate Scandal: Collusion, Conspiracy, and the Plot That Brought Nixon Down.* Washington, DC: Regnery Publishing, 2015.

## Videos

*I Have Never Forgotten You: The Life and Legacy of Simon Wiesenthal*, Moriah Films, Arnold Schwartzman. 2015.

*Janis: Little Girl Blue*, Columbia/Legacy, Amy Berg. 2015

*The Propaganda Game*, Memento Films, Alvaro Longoria. 2015.

*Soaked in Bleach*, Suburban Hitchhiker and Daredevil Films, Benjamin Statler. 2015.

# INDEX